GUY FREE, WORKING ON ME

A Woman's Journey to Self Awareness

Shauna Hoffman

BALBOA.
PRESS

A DIVISION OF HAY HOUSE

Balboa Press books may be ordered through booksellers or by contacting:

Balboa Press
A Division of Hay House
1663 Liberty Drive
Bloomington, IN 47403
www.balboapress.com
1-(877) 407-4847

Because of the dynamic nature of the Internet, any web addresses or links contained in this book may have changed since publication and may no longer be valid. The views expressed in this work are solely those of the author and do not necessarily reflect the views of the publisher, and the publisher hereby disclaims any responsibility for them.

The author of this book does not dispense medical advice or prescribe the use of any technique as a form of treatment for physical, emotional, or medical problems without the advice of a physician, either directly or indirectly. The intent of the author is only to offer information of a general nature to help you in your quest for emotional and spiritual well-being. In the event you use any of the information in this book for yourself, which is your constitutional right, the author and the publisher assume no responsibility for your actions.

Any people depicted in stock imagery provided by Thinkstock are models, and such images are being used for illustrative purposes only.
Certain stock imagery © Thinkstock.

Printed in the United States of America

ISBN: 978-1-4525-6638-2 (sc)
ISBN: 978-1-4525-6639-9 (e)
ISBN: 978-1-4525-6640-5 (hc)

Library of Congress Control Number: 2013900006

Balboa Press rev. date: 01/17/13

This Book is dedicated to all the amazing people in my life, both men and women who have taught me the lessons I share with my readers today. To my Husband I am thankful I can be Working On Me every day and you lovingly come along for the ride. To my beautiful Mother who taught me grace, compassion and strength, Szeretlek, I love you so. To my incredible nieces and Gbaby may your own personal journeys be gentle. To my Divine Friends, whom I cannot live without, thank you for traveling along with me, laughing and crying and learning how to just BE. And to my clients, thank you for letting me into your lives. Munchkins, remember there is no place like home.

Table of Contents

Chapter 1

It's My Turn!

WELCOME. THIS IS A great moment in your life—the moment when you have decided to stop taking care of everyone else and to start taking care of *you*! Stick with me and you will take the best ride of your life: one where *you* are the driver; *you* are in control. *Guy Free . . . Working On Me* is not meant to be a permanent lifestyle. It is meant to be a time in your life when you stop basing your worth, your happiness, and your self-esteem on whether or not you have a man at your side. This is going to be an all-out re-evaluation of who you are, who you want to be, and what you feel inside.

Are you ready? Take the wheel!

Let's start with how you came to pick up this book. You got dumped; divorce is on the horizon; you got yourself out of an unhealthy, codependent relationship; you have been widowed; you are currently in a relationship and somehow have lost yourself; or you have realized that until you work on *you*, you will never find your Soul Mate. So right here and now I say to you, if you don't find your OWN SOUL, how will you EVER find its mate?

A few years ago my niece showed up at my door ready to change her young 21-year-old life. She had just ended a very unhealthy, energy-sucking relationship and now had a new motto, "Boy Free, Working On ME." 21! Years ahead of the path that most of our sisterhood takes. With great female pride and definitely some ego, I applauded her wholeheartedly, "You go, girl!"

It was then that I realized that every woman I was seeing in my therapy practice at the time was going through the same thing. Dumper or dumpee, heartbroken or feeling free, each was in my office to find her "self" again. When I offered "Guy free, working on me" as their new motto, they all reacted with this huge sense of "DAMN RIGHT! It's my turn."

Many of you who are reading this book have been newly single-ized, as I call it. But, there is also another reader of this book that I welcome—the one who is still in a relationship yet has never taken the time to work on herself. "Guy Free, Working On Me" is a metaphor for understanding that you will never truly know yourself if your identity and belief in ultimate happiness is wrapped up in having a mate. Those of you in this part of the sisterhood will have it the toughest because you will be metamorphosing right in front of your man. That takes extra strength. Many men will not understand your new search for self. They will be scared or threatened and will try to keep you from changing. So for you ladies, it will take extra conviction to stay on your new path. The good news for some of you lucky women is that your mates will welcome this growth and come along on the ride with you.

Ladies, there are many catalysts to this change in perception, this switch from being outer-focused to being inner-focused. But they all really mean the same blasted thing: if you don't work on your "self," know your "self," honor your "self," then the inevitable will happen. You will wind up ending a relationship, someone else will end it, or you'll live in misery till-death-do-you-part. If you have not yet made the leap of faith towards YOU, I hope you take all that is here and choose once again.

What does it mean to work on your self? Don't you do that every day? After all, you are a living breathing being who is constantly growing and changing. This is true. But how you change, why you change, and what you change into is often too tied up in other people's beliefs, ethics, values, morals, needs, and desires. In other words, what THEY want you to be. Here you will learn to rethink who you are and who you want to present to the world based on

YOU, your innermost core self. Now, I know that sounds a little scary because, after all, most of us have never let that inner core show. You have masked it or, much more likely, you don't even know who the real you is! What we are going to explore here are your defense mechanisms, your patterns of relating to others, your ability to communicate what you really feel, and how you became who you are. And, if you LIKE this person! The goal? Genuine Self. Individuated Self. Self-Actualization. Authentic Self! All wonderful words for KNOWING YOUR "SELF."

The Work

Who am I now? For many of you, the first challenge is that some circumstance has put you in a position to redefine your identity—an identity that was maybe a little false in the first place. You were so-and-so's spouse, mother of three, the hot Porsche-driving CEO, or the engaged student studying to be the doctor that mom and dad always wanted in the family. When I ask someone in a therapy session to define herself, these are the kinds of descriptions I get: identities that come from outer circumstances, not from core beliefs or soul-minded thinking, titles given by those around you, by society.

How would you answer that question? If you said, "I am a kind yet often overly critical, definitely too giving, illogical thinker who loves people and wants to save the world," then you probably had a really great therapist or spiritual guide, or read a lot of self-help books!

Now let me make this clear, I won't be telling you how you should think or feel. From this point forward, we will be using a MODEL to look at you from the inside out, not the outside in. The model will help you look at how you feel about yourself, your life, and how you communicate your being to the world. You will work on your identity in terms of your personality, your style of communicating, your inner ego, your very deep psyche, and your true self-born soul. Don't ya love it?

It is a journey of SELF-discovery. You will be offered the opportunity to look at the three SELF'S: *Self-Awareness, Self-Esteem,* and *Genuine Self.* You will judge for yourself if your feelings, your communication process, and your self-image are healthy and, MORE IMPORTANTLY, in tune with your true beliefs. At the end of all of that we are going to find out what you are willing to change.

The Path of the Three Self's

We have all heard these phrases before—SELF-AWARENESS, SELF-ESTEEM, and GENUINE SELF—but I bet that most of you have never really given much thought to what each one means. These three phrases are the roots of self-learning and the tools to find peace in any relationship. So let's explore them a little bit!

1) SELF-AWARENESS is the awareness of self! You see, many of us work on remote control in life. We act and react and never take the time to really THINK about our existence. We never examine our choices, or even our behavior. We don't look at why we do what we do, we just do it. Becoming aware of what you think, the way you think, and the way you react in any given situation is the first step to becoming self-aware and seeing how you need to change. But it goes even deeper than that. Here is the fun part! Being self-aware means you know or are AWARE of what your dreams are, what your weaknesses are, what your strengths are, what your true loves are, and what you really feel deep inside.

Becoming aware of your automatic reactions and your defense mechanisms is both challenging and rewarding. For instance, are you guided by emotion or logic? Are you overly critical or overly accepting? Are you a pushover or are you rebellious? Do you know what you want to change about yourself? Do you know what it is about yourself that you want to keep? Have you ever taken the time or the energy to explore these things? This is the first step of this book. We are going to use the model to help you become self-aware! (More on the model later.)

2) SELF-ESTEEM. Esteem means "to like." Self-esteem means to like oneself. We often hear the phrase "Oh, she has low self-esteem." What low self-esteem really means is that someone has not yet found a way to honor herself. Instead she chooses to judge herself. There are many reasons for low self-esteem: non-nurturing parents, abusive relationships, learning disabilities, illness, etc. We cannot change the things that created the low self-esteem, but we can rethink how we want to live our lives, treat ourselves, and grow from this day forward!

By the end of this book I want to help all of you have not only self-esteem, but also SELF-LOVE!

3) GENUINE SELF. We have been talking about finding our true GENUINE SELF. But how do we know if we were already living a "genuine self" existence? Very good question. I like to do the easy litmus test. Take a look at your belief systems and see if what you present on the outside is what you really feel on the inside. You see, humans are like computers: we are programmed by the people and experiences in our lives. First by our parents, siblings, and nannies, then by the community we live in—our teachers, ministers, coaches, and friends. So ask yourself a few simple questions:

- Am I Jewish, Christian, Buddhist, etc., because this is what I truly believe? Or is it because my parents have taught me that this is who I am? Do I embrace this religion as a soulful part of me, or just as my heritage?
- Am I a Democrat, Republican, Liberal, Communist, etc., because these are my true political beliefs? Or did I get that voter card because my whole family would *kill* me if I didn't. I could never show up at Thanksgiving admitting I am not one of them.
- What are my beliefs about the roles of a woman? Do I even know what I think or have I taken on the conditioning of my mom, grandmother, and the lineage of female ancestors going back for centuries?

These few questions are just the start of looking within to find TRUE SELF. Understand, I won't be answering those questions for you. You will, once you have cleared the path of resistance to knowing YOU.

The Model For Change

I have been taunting you with that word for a few pages now. So what is THE MODEL? Well, it was first introduced by the famous psychoanalyst Eric Berne. It has been shared in many books and is taught and used by therapists worldwide. It is called Transactional Analysis, or TA. Big words for analyzing your transactions! I want to make it clear that I am not going to teach you textbook TA. I have taken the very hard work of thousands of therapists and made it as simple to share as possible! I have taken liberties with traditional terminology and concepts and phrased things differently. I want this to be the simplest and most straightforward approach for you to get to know your SELF. Purists might not be thrilled with me, but those of you reading this book will have the quickest and easiest way to grasp these brilliant life-changing ideas. Once you get the basics, TA is a giant world to explore further.

Let the party begin!

Chapter 2

The Self Love Movement!

BEFORE YOU START TO look at yourself, you have to learn to honor, spoil, and pamper YOU—judgment aside, guilt aside, ego aside. After all, how do you start to heal yourself if you don't honor yourself, if you don't find some level of kindness toward yourself? This chapter is where we are going to soften you! Then you will start to awaken your true spirit.

The Puppy

Imagine you have this new puppy—playful, excited, and energetic, but still a puppy. She has yet to learn to do things the right way. She gets into mischief and makes messes that you have to clean up. Here's the question: If you don't love this puppy, how are you ever going to take care of it? How are you going to get through the long process of puppyhood? You can't. Chances are you will be aggravated and judgmental and eventually you will stop training her. She will then be left outside in the backyard for the rest of her life.

Well, here is the sad truth. We do this to ourselves all the time. We judge ourselves, we stop loving ourselves, and then we stop working on ourselves. We become outcasts from our own life, just like the puppy. And then we wonder why we are not happy. AND we wonder why we don't have a relationship with someone who loves us, too.

Judgment Aside

Ladies, this chapter is a LOVE-FEST! I need you to find enough love and respect for yourself to do the work we are about to do. A moment when you believe you deserve the best in life, an honoring of self in order to change self. Here is the key. We are going to take judgment out of the equation for this chapter! Judgment is usually associated with negative feelings. We are going to stop judging ourselves . . . at least for now. That is until I show you how to do it in a healthy and productive way. But that's another chapter. For now we are going to practice kindness towards ourselves as we begin the real work.

Easy to say, right? But how do we do it? The best way to stop the self-criticism is to realize this simple truth: WE GOT TO WHERE WE ARE THE BEST WE KNEW HOW TO DO AT THE TIME. How simple is that? Really, if we knew how to have navigated those rough relationships and bad experiences in our lives better, we would have done it. Right? You see the *defense mechanisms* we have right now are the ones that seem like they serve us and protect us. That may have been true at one time in your life, but chances are they don't serve you anymore. The defense mechanisms that may have protected that 17-year-old you, may now be harming the 36-year-old you. They may still work with your family, but not with your lovers. Defense mechanisms are survival tools! But eventually we have to change them because, just like any tool, they get old and rusty and they have no purpose in our lives anymore.

So the first step to loving self is to stop labeling yourself and your life negatively. Most importantly, I need to help you see a very basic truth. We all make mistakes in our lives, make bad judgment calls, hurt those we love or allow those we love to hurt us. But the truth is: YOU DID THE BEST YOU KNEW HOW TO DO AT THE MOMENT. How could you have done any better if you weren't ready to look at yourself? How could you have done any better if you hadn't yet learned the right emotional and psychological tools? You couldn't. So now I want you to love yourself for who you were yesterday and who you want to be today. Say it aloud! "I DID THE BEST I KNEW HOW TO DO AT THE MOMENT!"

The Ladder

The ladies in my women's group call me "the storyteller." I love analogies to get the point across. So right now I will tell you the one that seems to make the most sense to my clients.

Imagine you are on a ladder to perfection. The top step is the goal. The top step means self-actualization; emotional health; world-honoring morals, ethics, and beliefs; selflessness; soul ascension. Many religions believe that this is our ultimate goal. Some would even say that when Christ said "come through me," he meant you must meet me on the top step. It is what Buddhists believe we reincarnate for, to come back over and over again until we reach a higher step on the ladder. Okay, let's not worry about the top step right now. Just remember that we are on a mission to eventual perfection.

Now look at the step you were on in your last relationship. And let's realize that when you got there, you found a buddy to hang with . . . your past lover. You two were on the same step at the same time. You had the same vibrations and the same energy. You were both as healthy as each other, and as unhealthy as each other. What? What does that mean? It means your behaviors, communication styles or beliefs, whether good or bad, fit with each other like puzzle pieces.

The fun part is that we are living-breathing-changing-ascending beings and, when we learn something new about ourselves, we take a step UP the ladder. So imagine that something happened in your life or in your relationship that gave you both a huge awakening. An *aha!* to better living. You both, together, got through that fight or through that life lesson and you both learned from it. Whatever it was, it made you both take a nice big step up the ladder. Now you are both together on a higher step than when you met. CONGRATULATIONS!

But sometimes in a relationship there is a time when we climb the ladder and our mate decides to stay where he is. I know we have all been there with men, friends, or even family. We have learned a better survival tool or have found ourselves on a search for a better understanding of ME. So, we find ourselves on a different step than they are on. It happens all the time: we each grow at a different pace and take those leaps to new levels at different moments in our life. In a relationship, as long as both of you are still going up the ladder, then that is all that matters. Maybe for a short time you are on the higher step, maybe he is. But you are both learning from each other and growing and changing and heading UP the ladder!

But what happens when we keep growing and our mate doesn't? What if he likes the step he is on? Is comfortable living that life? He doesn't want to know himself anymore, or grow anymore? You know what that feels like! Perhaps you have asked him over and over if he will go to therapy with you. Or you have quit drinking and he hasn't. Or you are back in school bettering your future and he wants your future to stay just where you are. What happens then? What do you do? Drag him up the ladder?

This is usually a very challenging time, when confusion and frustration can overtake you. If you want to keep him in your life, you have to go back down the step. You have to lower your vibration again. You have to go back to your old unhealthy reactions or actions. You have to stop moving up and move back down.

This is the opportunity for awakening: the moment when you say *I must love myself* and keep becoming a better, stronger, healthier human being even if he doesn't join me. I must be willing to leave him in order to become my genuine true self-actualized self. So what do you do? You honor YOU and take the step anyway.

This is self-love. It is telling yourself that it is okay to love yourself even if your mate don't join you.

Congratulate yourself, pet yourself, and honor yourself. I have news for you: when you master this lesson, you start flying up those stairs! You have just become the writer, editor, director, and star of the movie of your own life!

The PARTY!

So now I have taken away your opportunity to judge yourself, for now. Let's party! What I want you to do is to refresh yourself and have some fun! Heartache is too much to handle for very long. Worse, when you combine heartache with judgment, you become an emotional mess. So we will try some exercises in turning your focus from outer-focused to inner-focused, from past-focused to future-focused. That means no more mental time spent on *him*, or the last relationship. I know . . . I make it sound easy. Well, it sure is easier than the emotional roller coaster you have been on. You will resonate with some of these stories and exercises and others won't fit for you. That's okay. Do the ones that FIT! I am trying to get you to know yourself. These stories and exercises are the first step.

Hopefully ONE of them will give you the breakthrough that you may need to be comfortable SITTING WITH SELF.

EXERCISE: Facing Forward

Earlier, I presented the concept that you are going to help yourself move forward. You are taking the wheel. You are writing a new life for yourself. Let's see if you are ready.

FOLLOW THESE INSTRUCTIONS:
- Stand up and look straight ahead of you.
- Picture your incredible future, imagining everything that could make you happy and accepting the unknown as exciting and inviting.
- Take a nice big step forward!

Good. How does it feel? Now I want you to do it again.
- Stand up and look ahead at your unbelievable future.
- Now, with your body facing forward, turn your head back to look at him . . . behind you . . . only your head.
- Picture him and all of your relationship's history behind you.

- While you are looking behind you, try to take a step forward. You can't! Or if you can take the step, what does it feel like? My guess is you feel imbalanced and completely awkward. Do ya get it? You can't move forward when you are still focused on your past.
- Bring your head back to facing forward and look straight ahead. Center yourself again. Ground yourself.
- Now imagine everything beautiful, everything bad, and all that was in your past behind you. And picture it as a soft wind nudging you forward as you look ahead and see the amazing future that awaits you.
- Now take a nice big step!

As corny as it sounds, your past is the wind beneath your wings. Your past relationships, lessons, and life catapult you into the future. IF YOU LET THEM! This exercise is not meant to make you forget your past or ignore it; it is here to help you use your past to move into your future. Again, we can't go back and change the past. We can't change the choices we made, good or bad. But we can use our past energy and all that we learned or didn't learn to move us forward.

EXERCISE: Driving Forward

Here is another forward-facing exercise. Imagine you are driving on a city street. You are facing forward and driving ahead safely. Now imagine that while you are moving forward, you turn your head to look at what is behind you. You have your foot on the gas and you are in drive, but you are looking backwards. What happens? You swerve, you lose control, you CRASH!

This is what we do to ourselves when we are focused on our past while trying to move forward.

We do need to go in reverse sometimes, but there needs to be a conscious healthy reason for it. The only time we need to go in reverse is to change our direction ON PURPOSE! In other words, you make a conscious choice to look at your past in order to learn from it so that you can make a change and move forward in the present!

So ladies, the first step to moving forward is to face your future, not your past!

LET'S START THE AWAKENING . . .

The Red Jacket

One of my favorite life examples came from a woman who had been happily married for 40 years. Or so she thought. Then one shocking day her husband came home and told her he was leaving her for another woman. In the relationship, she had been a pure nurturer. She had spent their life together satisfying his needs and raising their kids. If he wanted chicken for dinner, they had chicken. If he wanted to watch football all day, she stayed at his side. She was constantly giving up her needs for his. So when she came into my office, heartbroken and deflated, I knew what we needed to do. We started the self-love movement! I asked her if there was anything that she had suppressed about herself over the years for him. Anything she loved to do, or wear, or be. And then she told me the STORY OF THE RED JACKET.

One day about 15 years ago, she made herself a beautiful red dress jacket. She worked really hard at picking the color of the material, designing it, cutting it, and then painstakingly sewing it to fit her perfectly. She loved it! This red jacket made her feel gorgeous and alive. She had handmade something that represented HER. And yep, you guessed it. HE hated it! It was too loud and too young-looking! He "forbid" her from wearing it. She was devastated. Always looking out for his needs instead of hers, she took that jacket and locked it away in her closet.

Yet something made her keep it. She kept it in her closet for 15 years, looking at it every few months. It was such a metaphor for the idea that she was actually keeping her true self locked away in a closet. She was keeping her true self hidden to keep him happy.

So at the end of our "Self-Love Movement" session, what do you think her homework was? WEAR IT! Wear that RED JACKET out to the store, to her friends house, to her kid's house. The next time she sees her ex, I want her to WEAR IT! Put that jacket on and feel gorgeous. And feel free. That's right, feel free of someone else telling you what you can and cannot do and, most importantly, who you can or cannot be.

This was a first step to her becoming an individual again. A first step to knowing how she defines herself. She defines herself as a RED JACKET-WEARING WOMAN! Her first moment of SELF-LOVE! From this moment, she redefined herself as an individual. She realized that she was one free-thinking soul who could make decisions about herself and for herself. And she looked DAMNED GOOD in that red jacket! I saw it!

The best part of this story is that four years later she came back to my office. In her 60's, she had found love again. She had found someone who honored her, admired her, and respected her. Why, ladies? Because she finally honored, admired, and respected herself!

Your Homework Assignment

The red jacket-wearing woman might not be you exactly. You might not be the nurturer or adaptive person who has given up too much for another. But I bet there is *something* that you gave up of yourself in order to keep your last mate happy. So, here is your homework assignment:

Find one thing that symbolizes what you gave up for the relationship. Then do it, wear it, live it, breathe it, be it!

Here are some examples from my clients:

- Go back to YOUR temple or church.
- Change your hair color.
- Eat your main meal at lunch.
- Join that Woman's Group.

- Wear miniskirts and bright red or those hippie jeans you loved, or that hot pink feminine tight blouse! Or those fuzzy rabbit slippers.
- Have that glass of wine.
- Repaint the house YOUR favorite color.
- Get that kitten you have always wanted! Or bird or elephant!
- Take that trip you have always dreamed of, the place HE didn't want to go.
- Get those acrylic nails. Or massage or facial.
- Spend money on YOU.
- Sign up for that class you always wanted.
- Go to that political rally.
- Call that friend of yours that he never liked.
- Go country line dancing, or salsa dancing, or TANGO!

This chapter was a self love-fest. Continue this work. Nurture yourself and pamper yourself. That is the only way you will love yourself enough to do the work we are about to do.

Chapter 3

Take Back Your Control

OKAY, NOW WE HAVE done the love-fest, so it's time for the reality check. The first step to taking back control of your life is to take responsibility for how you got here and how you are going to reach your ultimate happiness. It's time to look at yourself and tell the truth.

We are going to start utilizing a very strong muscle called the "logic muscle." Trust me, it will have its very own chapter later on, but it is much needed right now to make the SHIFT you need in order to grow. We are going to help you look at yourself with logic—unemotional attachment and FACTS!

I cannot tell you how important this chapter is to facilitate you growing into the most healthy, happy person you can be. What I am going to ask you to do is be honest with yourself about who you are, who you have been, and who you want to be. You will need to do this in order to do the work in this book. If you lie to yourself, hide your flaws from yourself, you will never be able to let those flaws be released forever from your life.

Here is the good news: you are not doing this in public; you are reading this book all by yourself. I am not asking you to admit your flaws to others. I am going to open up in you a place of truth where it is okay to admit to yourself, "I am not perfect. I have made mistakes. I may have hurt others and I may have hurt myself. I know there are parts of me that I want to change."

The payoff? PEACE. Really! When you finally admit to yourself things your subconscious already knows, you experience this incredible level of peace in your soul. Remember what we learned as children: when we tell a lie, we have to tell so many more just to keep the lie alive. So when we lie to ourselves about our faults or our choices or our feelings, we have to create a whole world of lies to keep up our "false face." It gets tiring. It causes a level of confusion in our souls that brings us unhappiness and depression. And worst of all, it is hard work to ignore our own reality. I will say it again: IT IS HARD WORK TO IGNORE OUR OWN REALITY.

There are many woman out there who have a heyday judging themselves and telling the world how flawed they are. That in itself is a flaw. This chapter is not about admitting to the world all that is wrong with you and how unworthy you are. I am talking about the opportunity to non-judgmentally, introspectively, look at your communication processes, your defense mechanisms, and your personality traits to see what you feel needs to change. A matter of fact, I don't want you to tell a soul about your progress until you finish the book. You see, as we work on one side of us, another side of us will change. By the end, what you learn in one chapter may not even have validity anymore.

How do we make that mental shift to look at ourselves logically? Two words: WILLINGNESS and RELEASE.

Willingness

Let's start with WILLINGNESS. The dictionary describes the word *willing* as "ready to act gladly or easily compliant." That is what I am hoping you can find—an openness and level of joy in looking at yourself. If you come into the next chapters defending yourself all the way, you will never grow.

Say it out loud:

I AM NOW WILLING AND OPEN TO JOYFULLY AND NON-JUDGMENTALLY LOOK AT MY PAST BEHAVIOR, MY DEFENSES, AND MY EMOTIONAL RESPONSES. I AM NOW READY FOR CHANGE!

I have spoken a lot about defense mechanisms. Let's talk about one of the strongest defense mechanisms we have—ANGER. This can be anger at others, anger at a situation, and anger at ourselves. "I am so angry that they did that to me. I am so angry that they made such a stupid choice." Or, "I am so angry that this happened to me." Or, "I am so angry at myself that I let this person do this to me."

Anger has its place. It is one of the best defense mechanisms that we have to defend ourselves against future harm. It usually throws us into an extremely strong and highly reactive state of protection. When we are angry, we usually push away the person or thing that has hurt us. We put up a wall. Even if we have the opportunity to express that anger at the person who has harmed us, the anger is usually coming from a place of protection rather than a place of healing. This emotional state is not a place of resolution, but a state of explosion and then maybe catharsis. And this is why . . . THE EMOTIONAL STATE OF ANGER IS JUST A COVER FOR THE DEEPER STATE OF SADNESS, HURT, OR PAIN.

When we are angry with someone, something, or at ourselves, what is usually underlying that emotion is sadness. "I am so sad that this happened to me. I am so sad that he did this to me. I am so sad that he chose to leave me. I am so sad that I sabotaged that relationship. I am so sad that I did this to myself." Or hurt. "I am so hurt by what you did. I am so hurt by the choices that you made." Anger is just a cover for something much deeper.

A very large piece of the work of this chapter is to be *willing* to look at what we are angry at, then try to peel away the anger to reveal the pain or sadness or hurt that is connected to the situation or person. Then we can change the perception from anger to the real emotion involved. By doing this step we take ourselves out of a state of defensiveness and put ourselves in a state of dealing with the deeper emotion. And once we deal with it, we can heal it.

Release

Remember what we learned in the last chapter? You did the best you could do at the time. Now I am going to offer you a new revelation: You did the best you knew how to do at the time AND *so did everyone else around you.*

WHAT? You mean I am telling you to stop blaming the other people around you? *Ahhh*, that doesn't seem right, does it? After all, all those guys did you wrong! Especially that last one! He cheated on me, he's an alcoholic, he stole my money, he didn't honor me, he didn't care about me, and on and on. But here's the rub—you accepted that level of humanity into your life. It's not his fault. It's yours. And I say that LOVINGLY!

In order to get past the pain, the anger, and the sadness and get to our healing, we have to accept this fact. We did the best we knew how to do at the time and so did everyone around us.

When we judge others, we are again outer-focused and not looking at ourselves. You see, very often we do realize that the people around us are hurting us, but in the end, it is up to US to get out of an unhealthy place. Or it is up to us to take the control back in our life. They can't do it. So what good does it do to blame them? You handed them the wheel. But again, *it was the best you knew how to do in the first place.* Now you know better. You are here. You are on your path to healing. So that tells me that there is an ounce of love in you for you. Congratulations! Pet it, honor it, and let's help it to grow.

Most importantly, when you spend mental time and physical energy judging the people that hurt you, it only hurts you more. You know what it feels like when you're having a great day and then you see something or hear something that reminds you of him? All of a sudden the judgment and the anger take you over and there goes your wonderful day. It grows with every thought until you have this pit in your stomach. Okay ladies, I am now offering you the opportunity to take back your control!

EXERCISE: Take Back Your Control

In this exercise you will take someone that you believe hurt you badly and see if you can release your pain, anger, and judgment about that person. Though I could write a whole book about this, we are just going to take a small step today towards self-awareness. Take out a pen and paper and start journaling about the three requests I am making of you. Write as much as you need to mentally accomplish the goal in each step, or find some understanding of the importance of the step, even if only superficially for now. You might not totally believe it yet, but we are getting your mind set for healing. If you are not a person who likes to journal, then talk to yourself out loud. Write, scribble, scream, or whisper as you attempt the following:

1. Accept responsibility for your piece of the relationship and for *choosing to be there.* Gently ask yourself questions, like the following: What did I do to provoke the situation? Why did I stay and not get out earlier? What was the best part of staying? Why was I afraid to leave? What was my weakness in this situation?

2. DON'T blame yourself or judge yourself, just *lovingly accept responsibility.* Now that you have looked at your piece of the relationship, take the judgment out of it. As you see your piece of the drama, you may decide it's time to blame yourself or be angry at yourself. That won't help. I just want you to take responsibility for your choices from a logical, nonjudgmental place. And then state this FACT over and over until you get it. "I did the best I knew how to do at the moment."

3. Now *let the anger at the other person or judgment towards yourself go!* And *thank yourself for finally moving FORWARD!* If you have really done step two, then you will now be at a much more peaceful place about yourself and the situation. So in this step I want you to release the pain, *release the past.* Let it go! See it float away. Now pet yourself for the work you have just done. And thank yourself for gaining some new awareness of SELF!

If you need to do these exercises ten times before moving on to the next chapter, then do so. My wish for you is that you can find a level of peace with your past in order to start changing your future.

Chapter 4

The Path To Freedom

THE LAST CHAPTERS HAVE hopefully opened your mind to the first few steps needed for CHANGE. We have looked at what made you decide it was time for change in your life. We have helped you take some level of responsibility for how you got to where you are in life. We have helped you find the WILLINGNESS to look deeper at yourself in order to facilitate change. Now the real work is HOW TO CHANGE into a healthy, balanced, self-aware and happy woman!

Sybil In My Head

Do you ever notice that you usually have more than one voice screaming in your head? They are all your voices, but each voice leads you to a different reaction to a situation or to a different choice in life. Do you notice that one voice is usually louder than the others? These are what TA calls "ego states." These are what I am going to call the five sides of your personality. It is these five personality states that you need in balance to live a drastically happy life. It is from these five sides that we think, communicate, act, and feel. These are the five sides of your personality that we are going to investigate, dissect, remold, and renew. These are the five sides of your personality that when renewed will help you feel happy and healthy—dare I say the words—with or without a man! You might have heard some of this terminology before: Critical Parent State, Nurturing Parent State,

Free Child State (Often Rebellious), Adaptive Child State, and Adult State.

Here is how it works . . .

The Alarm Clock

Imagine you have to set your alarm to wake up in time to go to work the next day. You need to be there by 9 a.m. Here is how the five voices in your head argue:

1. The Critical Parent voice in your head says, "You are such a lousy worker and everyone knows it. You have been late and lazy and doing a horrible job this last week. You better set your alarm for 6:30, put on something much more professional to wear, get there by 8:30, work through lunch, and prove that you are not the bum everyone thinks you are." And so you set the alarm for 6:30.

2. The Nurturing Parent voice says, "Oh, you've had such a very stressful week! Why don't you sleep in, set the alarm for 8, grab a Starbucks on the way to work, and get there around 10. Be gentle on yourself today and maybe even quit work at 4, stop on the way home and get that massage you have wanted. You deserve it!" And so you set the alarm for 8:00 a.m.

3. The Free Child voice says, "You know what? I'm not going to work today! I'm going to the beach, then to the mall! I don't want to be locked inside today. I'm tired. I know that they need that report from me, but I don't care. I'm sleeping in. Yep, I'm not setting the alarm at all!" And so you never set the alarm.

4. The Adaptive Child voice says, "Oh, I am such a lousy worker. I wish everyone liked me more. I really am not worthy of this job. I am so sorry I am not a better person. I think I will set the alarm for 6, get there by 7:30, do all my work, start on Keith's work and Craig's work, and work really, really hard until 6! My boss will be so proud

of me and then everyone will really love me!" And you set the alarm for 6 a.m.

5. <u>The Adult</u> voice says, "In order to be at work at 9, I will set the alarm for 7, be out of my shower by 7:12, make my bed by 7:18, be dressed and downstairs by 7:32, eat a balanced breakfast by 8:02, get gas by 8:21, and be at work by 8:55." So you set the alarm for 7 a.m.

Does one of these voices sound more familiar to you than the others? Or do you hear one voice one day and the next day you hear another? The most important thing is we need ALL of these voices, but we need them to be balanced and used at the appropriate times in our lives. Sometimes we need the Critical Parent to kick our butts into gear. Sometimes we *are* working too hard and not taking care of ourselves, so we need the Nurturing Parent voice to speak up. Sometimes we need to take a day off and have some fun. You see, all of these personality states have a positive use in our lives. But what happens when they get imbalanced is that the negative traits of one personality state seem to rule over the others. Hence the work we are going to do for the rest of this book.

We are going to look at each one of these voices in your head and become aware of which ones are out of balance. Which voice is louder and which voice is too weak. We are going to really look hard at the positive traits of each personality state and the negative sides of each state. We are going to look deeply at ourselves so that we can learn new tools to communicate, live, and breathe from a healthier place.

Are you ready?

Let's take a closer look. In each state there are what I call positive attributes and negative attributes. It is when we come too often from the negative attributes that we feel the imbalance.

Shauna Hoffman

The Fab Five

CRITICAL PARENT

NEGATIVE ATTRIBUTES	POSITIVE ATTRIBUTES
Negative	Protector
Controlling	Sets Boundaries
Opinionated	Enforces Values
Confrontational	Sense Of Power
Critical	Good Critic

NURTURING PARENT

NEGATIVE ATTRIBUTES	POSITIVE ATTRIBUTES
S/Mothering	Feel Needed
Others, Not Self	Self-Care
Self-Care Is Selfish	Healing
Blinded To Others' Faults	Selfless Giving

REBELLIOUS/FREE CHILD/FREE CHILD

NEGATIVE ATTRIBUTES	POSITIVE ATTRIBUTES
No I Won't!	Rocks Boat For Change
All About Me!	Not Guilt-Driven
I Don't CaRe!	Stands Up For Self
Very Emotional	Has A Voice!
Overly Impulsive	Creative
Few Boundaries	Free-Spirited
Too Free-Spirited	Light-Hearted
Action/No Fear Of Consequences	Spontaneous

ADAPTIVE CHILD

NEGATIVE ATTRIBUTES	POSITIVE ATTRIBUTES
Helpless	Adaptable To Change
Submissive	Not Too Invested In Result
Seeks Approval	Trusting
Guilt-Driven	Admits When Wrong
Never Gets Angry	Able To Ask For Help
Too Vulnerable	

ADULT

Negative Attributes	Positive Attributes
I'm Thinking	Objective
Too Analytical	Good On The Job
Too Unemotional	Balanced Decision-Making
Not Spontaneous	Balanced Emotions
Decisions Based On Logic	Uses Logic To Advantage, Not Feelings

Take a look at this chart. You will notice the five states are split between three circles. This is a HEALTHY person's chart. With five healthy states, a chart it would look like this.

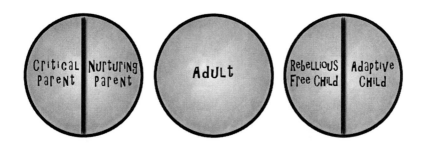

The parent state would be split in half—one-half Critical Parent, one-half Nurturing Parent. The child state would be split in half—one-half Rebellious/Free Child, one-half Adaptive Child. The Adult state is all on its own. A full circle! This means we need twice as much healthy adult thinking and feeling as we do the other states.

In each of the following chapters we will investigate one of the above personality states. It will be your job to be as honest as possible with yourself to see which states rule you and where your imbalances are. More than likely, you already have some ideas. We will also do some work to see how you cultivated these states. Remember, so much of our communication and thought processes were programmed into us. We will not only look at you, but at some of the caretakers and family members in your life to see how you have been programmed and by whom. It is a fascinating journey! Hopefully by the end you will find some clarity into who you are now, and how you got here. We are all works in progress, so let's start the PROGRESS!

And remember; let's start with WILLINGNESS.

Chapter 5

The Critical Parent State

CRITICAL PARENT

NEGATIVE ATTRIBUTES	POSITIVE ATTRIBUTES
NEGATIVE	PROTECTOR
CONTROLLING	SETS BOUNDARIES
OPINIONATED	ENFORCES VALUES
CONFRONTATIONAL	SENSE OF POWER
CRITICAL	GOOD CRITIC

OFTEN WHEN WE THINK of the word *critical*, it brings up negative emotions. But this personality state is truly the one that empowers us, gives us strength, and sets boundaries for our lives. I call it the Mama Bear/Papa Bear side of us. It's the "should, must, have to" finger-pointing voice inside our head. We use the Critical Parent (CP) piece of our thought process to make decisions that protect us. However, when we overuse or rely too much on this side, we become highly critical of others and, even worse, highly critical of ourselves. It's the state that instead of saying, "Hmm, don't wear that dress, it's not flattering," says, "Don't wear that dress, you look fat." It's the state that likes to control situations and likes to control others.

To best describe the positive and negative attributes of this personality state, we will look at two different definitions of the word CRITICAL. Here is a definition to help you understand the positive side of the word: *Using skillful judgment to discern the truth.*

Now here is a definition to help you understand the negative side: *Readily inclined to find fault and judge with severity, often way too readily, and not based on solid facts.*

One of these is balanced "critical thinking" and the other is imbalanced critical thinking. You see, when we overuse our CP, we become *unnecessarily judgmental* and oftentimes lose the "facts" concerning the person, place, or thing that we are critiquing. UNFORTUNATELY, it is usually ourselves that we are critiquing.

For instance, our balanced CP voice might say, "You have gained five pounds and you must lose it to stay healthy." Our imbalanced judgmental CP voice would say, "You are so fat, no one will ever want to be with you again." Do you hear the difference? The person with an unhealthy CP will damage themselves by being so critical of their choices, their body, and their work that they destroy their own self-esteem.

Now you have a quick overview of the positive and negative attributes of CP. Let's take a little closer look at each.

The Positive Attributes

On the positive side of this state, let's replace the word *critical* with the word *critic*. A critic is someone who judges, evaluates, and analyzes something. The important word here is "judges." On the positive side of Critical Parent, we use our best critic within us to judge a situation and then take the action we need to give us control, empower us, and protect us. The "should–must–have to" side of us is desperately needed. It's the piece of us that sets boundaries. It's the side of us that enforces our values and morals. It's also the side of us that critiques others AND OURSELVES in a positive, constructive way.

A *boundary* is something that creates your personal space, a line that you draw to make you feel safe. When you think of personal boundaries, you need to think of a line you draw to tell people how they can and cannot treat you. It is created by you and enforced by you. It is a message you send to everyone around you to let them know the kind of treatment you accept from others and the kind of treatment you do *not* accept. Your boundaries act as your armor and your shield. It is with your boundaries that you protect yourself.

Let's take a look at a few statements that represent good, strong, healthy boundaries. By cultivating boundaries like the following statements, we protect ourselves against allowing others to harm us.

Examples of Boundary Statements:

1. Do not yell at me. Please speak to me respectfully.
2. Do not call me names. If you want to communicate to me without name-calling, I will listen.
3. Do not take advantage of me. If you give back to me as much as I give to you, then we can have a healthy relationship.
4. Do not take me for granted. I am happy to be a part of your life as long as you appreciate me.
5. The choices you are making about your life are now affecting my life. I need to rethink if these are helping or hurting my life.
6. Do not tell me what I can or cannot do, whom I can see, what I can wear, or where I can go. You do not control my life, I do.
7. Do not tell me what I am supposed to believe or think. I am mySELF.

These are just a few of the myriad of boundaries you need to cultivate to protect yourself. Once you are aware of healthy boundaries, your next step is to use your Critical Parent side to make judgments about people or situations to see if they are good for you or bad for you. You can see from just these few statements that when you use your positive Critical Parent side to make these judgments to protect yourself, you are in turn setting good strong healthy boundaries. And *vice versa*. When you set good strong healthy boundaries for yourself, you are in turn protecting yourself from being hurt by others. A win/win situation!

The next positive attribute of the Critical Parent is that we use this side of us to enforce our morals, ethics, and values—the things that we believe on which we base the actions of our lives. The CP side of us is the ENFORFCER of these choices. The SHOULD, MUST, HAVE TO. "I should not steal. I should not lie. I must be a good person. I must work hard. I have to take care of myself. I have to pay my way. I cannot cheat on this test." Life tempts us with many choices. It is the CP side that keeps us from making choices that go against what we really believe in, or what is right for us. Every time we use our Critical Parent in a healthy way to enforce our values, our self-image becomes stronger. We like what we see in ourselves. We become EMPOWERED. We become individuated.

I love the next piece of the CP—EMPOWERMENT. The CP is the side that gives us a sense of power in a situation, or just in life. Now this is an interesting idea: Power. As we know from history, books, and movies, power can be used for good or for evil. Obviously when it is used by the POSITIVE side of our CP, it is used for good. Our OWN good! The challenge that many women have is they feel that when they harness and exert their power, they are either negating their feminine side or are presenting themselves in an unfeminine way. In many cases, they are just NOT COMFORTABLE with this side of their character.

This is a major piece of work for many women. It is a glorious day when we can access our sense of power with surety and with grace. Meaning, we still hold onto all that is feminine about us, but we stand strong in our convictions and our beliefs. You see, by finding our sense of empowerment, we find the strength to assert ourselves. We use our assertiveness to stand up for our needs, wants, and our deepest desires. In other words, we use our own power and our own strength to stand strong for SELF. The beauty is that the more we practice this side of our thinking, the more empowered we become! It is a beautiful circle of growth.

Knowing your needs, standing up for your needs, asserting your truth is EMPOWERING. The more you do so, the more empowered you become.

Now let's take a look for a moment at what happens when these parts of our CP are imbalanced.

The Negative Attributes

Negative Attributes	Positive Attributes
Negative	Protector
Controlling	Sets Boundaries
Opinionated	Enforces Values
Confrontational	Sense Of Power
Critical	Good Critic

The first thing that happens is that we become extremely critical of others and opinionated in life. We become bullies. We push others to see our side of things. We become confrontational. We judge situations with no balance. Oftentimes our scale is set so wrong that we are mean and abusive in the things we say and think. Even worse, they are often not based in fact. The out-of-balance CP voice is a very harsh voice to use on others. The most important piece of this is that it is usually used in conjunction with another side of Critical Parent—CONTROL. We use the harsh, critical, opinionated, bullying side of us to control others. If we can put someone down enough, or make them feel weak, then we can control them. We all have known people like that in our life. For many of you it was a boss. For others it was a parent or a mate. But for some of you, it's you!

We all have the capability to practice these unhealthy sides. Your job now is to see how you stand on the CP scale. Are you balanced? Are you overly critical? Or, like many women, are you lacking in the healthy Critical Parent attributes all together? Here is something to consider: some people are only critical of others with NO criticism of themselves, while others are never critical of others, but are constantly critical of themselves. And some are always critical of others and just as critical of themselves. Some have such a small Critical Parent that they do not have any CP attributes at all. Where do you fall? Use your Critical Parent side—with gentleness—to evaluate yourself and answer these questions.

THE CRITICAL PARENT QUESTIONAIRE

1. Do I judge myself from a balanced state or am I cruel to myself?
2. Do I allow people in my life to hurt me over and over again, or do I set good boundaries with others?
3. Do I feel more comfortable around people who judge me or do they make me uncomfortable?
4. Do I sometimes judge others excessively without due reason?
5. Is my first instinct to take control of a situation or to let others control it?
6. Am I willing to give up control when necessary and still be happy?
7. Have I given up control over parts of my life that I regret?
8. Are any of the people in my life abusive towards me?
9. Are there any people I am abusive to?
10. Do I seem to be unnecessarily opinionated about people, things, and circumstances?
11. Do I try to bully others into thinking the way I think?
12. Do I let others bully me into thinking the way they think?
13. Am I often critical of others with NO criticism of myself?
14. Am I rarely critical of others, but constantly critical of myself?

15. Am I always critical of others and just as critical of myself?

Final Assessment of Your Critical Parent

Look at how you answered the above questions and then look at the chart of positive and negative Critical Parent attributes below.

CRITICAL PARENT

NEGATIVE ATTRIBUTES	POSITIVE ATTRIBUTES
NEGATIVE	PROTECTOR
CONTROLLING	SETS BOUNDARIES
OPINIONATED	ENFORCES VALUES
CONFRONTATIONAL	SENSE OF POWER
CRITICAL	GOOD CRITIC

Now ask yourself:
1. Is my Critical Parent state too weak, having very few positive attributes?
2. Is my Critical Parent state too strong, having mostly negative attributes?
3. Do I feel I have a healthy and balanced Critical Parent state, expressing and believing mostly the positive attributes of Critical Parent and rarely going over to the negative attributes side of the chart?

The last step in looking at the Critical Parent State is looking at how it affects your relationships. Let's look at your relationships to see where you stand.

Your relationships with MEN:
1. Do you find men who are critical of you?
2. Do you find men who are judgmental?
3. Do you find men who are controlling?
4. Do you find men who are bullies or confrontational?

5. Do you find men who are OVERLY opinionated?

Next we are going to take a look at how you were programmed by your upbringing. Remember, we are like blank slates when we are born and then the programming begins. Well, I want you to take a look at your parents and see who is critical and who is not. Are they both critical? Are they healthy balanced CP's or is one or both imbalanced?

Was one or both of your parents:
1. Critical of you?
2. Judgmental of others and situations?
3. Overly controlling of you, of others?
4. Confrontational bullies to you or to others?
5. Overly opinionated?
6. Did your parents share their morals and ethics with you?
7. Did they live, by example, the same morals and ethics they taught you?

In Chapter 11 we will explore this further. But for now I just want you to have an idea how you may have been influenced.

There are many relationships in our lives that enforce the Critical Parent. Often bosses are put in that position, and teachers and parents, of course. But the question is whether they are balanced and using their positive CP or are they imbalanced and overusing their CP, coming at you or others from a cruel, abusive, controlling, or judgmental place? Remember, we need this CP state to be HEALTHY! Imagine what we would be like if we did not use the word "should" in our lives. Would we really get up and go to work? Would we go to the gym or take that walk? Would we eat the healthy foods we need to keep us strong? Or would we be hanging around all day watching TV, eating chocolate, and wasting our lives away? What if we did not have a voice in our head that gave us our morals? Would we lie? Would we cheat? Would we steal? Would we even know that we

SHOULDN'T? This is a normal healthy side of our psyche, but we need it BALANCED!

More importantly, we need it balanced so that we use our Critical Parent to choose the most important relationships in our lives. Imagine a mate, friend, or a parent that says there is something you need to change about yourself, but they say it with love instead of cruelty. How lovely it would be to have that mate want to protect us and keep us safe from harm. How amazing it would be to have our mate be able to critique himself and make changes, so that you do not have to be his judge and jury. Now that is healthy.

Here is the *real* work. How amazing would it be for you to critique yourself with love instead of cruelty? How much growth would it be for you to learn to set boundaries and protect yourself from people or situations that cause you emotional or physical harm? How positive would your relationships be if you could bring that positive Critical Parent to all of your relationships without seeming like their judge and jury?

That is the work of the CRITICAL PARENT.

Chapter 6

The Nurturing Parent State

NURTURING PARENT

Negative Attributes	Positive Attributes
S/Mothering	Feel Needed
Others Not Self	Self Care
Self-Care Is Selfish	Healing
Blinded To Others Faults	Selfless Giving

IMAGINE THE PARENT CIRCLE cut perfectly in half. One side would be the healthy Critical Parent and the other side would be the healthy Nurturing Parent. Both sides would appear perfectly equal because we need both personality states to live a healthy existence.

The Nurturing Parent (NP) voice is usually one of the most comfortable voices for women. We tend to be brought up believing that women are supposed to take care of others' needs first and foremost. We are the nurturing sex. We nurture others, raise the children, and heal the world. When you think of the word "nurture," you usually think of a woman. So, as I start to describe the Nurturing Parent voice, women will usually be able to relate to it. That is until I ask them how they nurture themselves!

The Positive Attributes

Let's start by looking at the positive attributes of the NP. One of the best words associated with NP is the word CARING. When you nurture others, you are caring for others. There is a special part of our minds, hearts, and souls that is gratified and fed by giving selflessly. It is the concept of selfless giving that makes it truly nurturing. Caring is often done in a physical form, but that is not the only part of NP. Caring in an emotional way makes up the biggest Nurturing Parent part of us. The NP cares if someone is happy or if they are healthy. The NP cares if someone is in need. The NP is known for looking outside of themselves at someone else's needs, often to the point of self-sacrifice.

One of the best reasons that people, male or female, like to nurture others is because of the emotional payback we get. It's a BIG ONE! It makes us feel needed. When we give to others, it gives us a sense of worth. To feel like someone needs us is one of the payoffs of being human. We are not hermits living in the woods. A part of fitting into society is finding our place in it. For many women, our place is a place where we can give. But that is part of the danger of an unhealthy NP. When we give to others to the point where we sacrifice our own needs, when we give to others when they don't want it, and when we feel guilty taking care of ourselves, we have crossed over to the UNHEALTHY NURTURING PARENT!

The Unhealthy NP

I am going to break this down and explain the unhealthy side of an NP. It is this skewed idea that some women have that says SELF-CARE IS SELFISH. Woman so often come into my practice and share with me that they feel guilty taking care of their needs. They feel selfish asking to go to their favorite restaurant for dinner. They feel guilty buying things for themselves. They feel selfish resting when others need them. Again, they have crossed over to the unhealthy side of NP and believe that *self-care is selfish!*

So I want you to ask yourself a few questions:

1. Do you take your wants into consideration when you make decisions with others? Or are you likely to defer to their desires rather than your own?
2. Does it make you happier to make others happy then to make yourself happy?
3. Do you feel selfish speaking up and asking for your needs to be met?
4. Do you take as much physical care of yourself as you do others in your life?

Here is a typical woman's unhealthy NP scenario. She comes into my office exhausted and angry with herself because she is overweight. She tells me that at dinnertime, she designs the menu around what her kids want and what her husband likes. She does not have time to make huge salads for herself as the kids won't eat it, her hubby wants pasta, and it takes too long to make dinner for everyone and herself. So guess who doesn't get what she wants? Guess who is much more likely to spend an hour making their meals than spending ten minutes to make her own? Guess where she lands on the unhealthy NP chart? Now wait a minute. You say she is nurturing others? That means she is a *good* NP. NO! She is sacrificing her needs to take care of others. SHE HAS CROSSED OVER TO THE UNHEALTHY SIDE!

We hear the words *co-dependent* a lot. Part of co-dependence is when we get something out of giving up something. In this case, the woman was fulfilling her need to feel wanted by her family by giving up her own health. This is one of the hardest concepts for me to get through to women: sometimes it is OKAY to put your needs ahead of other people's needs. After all, once you are gone, who will take care of them? SELF-CARE IS A WONDERFUL THING!

Here is one of my favorite analogies . . .

The glass

Imagine you are a glass of energy. Every time you nurture someone, imagine you are pouring your energy from your glass into his or her glass. You pour your energy into your mate, into your kids, into your friends, into your work, into your parents. My question to women all the time is, "who pours their energy into you?" Often they look at me with a blank stare and say, "My kids sometimes, my mate once in a while, my friends usually." My next question is, "Do you LET others pour their energy into you, or do you say, 'No bother, I am fine?'" Guess what the answer is! This is the female unhealthy nurturer syndrome. We pour and pour and pour ourselves into others and smile and say "no thank you" when others offer to pour their energy into us. What happens eventually? Your glass is EMPTY! You are exhausted and angry, resentful and depressed. Why? Because you truly believed you did not need nurturing from others. You did not want to put anyone out by asking for help. You did not believe you were as worthy of receiving as the people you gave to. And then you were left on empty. Here and now, learn how to RECEIVE! Understand that you need to be nurtured and let others nurture you. And most of all learn how to nurture yourSELF!

Make a list right now of ways you nurture yourself in the present. Then I want you to add to it. Here are some hints:
- I go to lunch with my girlfriends.
- I get a massage, or manicure, or hairstyle.
- I take long walks in the sun.

- I do my exercises.
- I take dance classes, or art or sailing lessons.
- I meditate, read, sleep, eat properly.

Make your list now. Then come up with ten more ways to add to it in the very near future.

Negative Attributes

Here is one more trait from the negative side of Nurturing Parent that I want to bring your attention to: "mothering becomes smothering." Often a nurturer enjoys taking such good care of others that she smothers them. It's the typical trait of women in new relationships. A woman likes to nurture a new man and make him think she has the best of the female nurturer traits! She thinks by doing and doing for this new man that she will be endeared to him. WRONG! Usually it is the first thing that turns a guy off. Or if it doesn't turn him off, RUN—he has a very unhealthy need for a mother in his life! Sadly, this is the role that many women take on in their relationships—the role of nurturer and mother to their mate. Then they come to me and say, "He never does anything for me. Why do I have to ask for him to notice if *I* need something? Why does he do so much for his friends and the neighbors and his secretary and not for me?" My answer is, "You trained him that way!" Put another way, "you found someone who matched your unhealthy Nurturing Parent state and you kept him." The good news is you are reading this book and YOU CAN CHANGE!

Another unhealthy imbalanced use of this state of supposed nurturing is to CONTROL people. What, you say? But that is Critical Parent. Yes it is. Some people use nurturing as a tool to control others into needing them. It is extreme passive-aggressive behavior. It's when you use your nurturing side to make others feel GUILTY, so guilty that they have to accept your nurturing and mold to what you want them to be. Often people are so sweet and giving that the other person feels trapped into a relationship, or into a situation. Have you ever had someone so smotheringly sweet ask you to do something that you don't want to do? But just the fact that they are so sweet makes you feel too guilty to turn them down? That is UNHEALTHY NP.

This leads me to the last piece of an unhealthy NP, which is the opposite end of the guilt spectrum. This is when you are so overly nurturing that you tend to become blinded to others' faults. This thought process in woman leads her to make excuses for her man's behavior instead of seeing that there is something that is just not right for her with this man. It goes back to the other half of parent state, the Critical Parent. You are so nurturing, caring, and loving to that person that you refuse to be critical enough to see the issues that are staring you right in the face. Your Nurturing Parent is too big and your Critical Parent is too small.

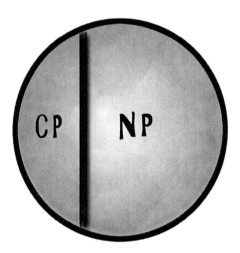

Your Relationships

So take a look at your relationships now. I want you to list the names of some of the closest people in your life. Then I want you to think of the GLASS. I want you to write down who pours into you and how much. And who you pour into and how much. I want you to see where the imbalances are. I want you to decide if you are part of the problem in these imbalances and you need to ask for more. Or is it so imbalanced that you need to stop pouring?

Of course, there are some people and instances that call for imbalance. As a parent we usually will pour more into our kids while they are young than they pour into us. That is normal. But check the balance once they grow up! This should have changed. If you have someone who is ill in your life, chances are you are pouring much more into them than they can pour into you. That is okay as long as you are finding other ways to get that glass filled—with other people or through taking really good care of yourself! The idea is to make sure your glass stays full no matter how much you give to whom! SELF-CARE IS NOT SELFISH . . . IT IS NECESSARY TO MAKE YOUR WORLD GO AROUND!

So here is the wrap-up on the two parent states: you need both a Nurturing Parent and a Critical Parent. And you need them healthy and working hand-in-hand in your thought processes, actions, relationships, and life!

You've heard the saying that *opposites attract.* Well, it's true when it comes to relationships and your parent states. Usually people with unhealthy Critical Parent states are attracted to unhealthy Nurturing Parents and *vice versa.* Picture it. You have the gentle, giving nurturer with the critical, powerful leader. After all, imagine how long two overly critical people would last together? The power struggles and the unending criticism would cause both people to throw up their strong CP boundaries and call it quits. And how often do you see two Nurturing Parents in a relationship? The unending niceness and desire to please each other creates a stalemate. As we said in this chapter, NP's have a hard time accepting nurturing from someone else, so it is rare to see two overly nurturing people in a relationship with each other.

Please understand that I am talking about people who are unhealthy in these two states. A perfect world is when both people in a relationship have a healthy Critical Parent and a healthy Nurturing Parent. Then two halves do make a whole!

Here is a graphic of what your parent state should look like:

Chapter 7

The Rebellious/Free Child State

JUST AS THE PARENT state has two halves, so does the child state. Half is the Rebellious/Free Child and half is the Adaptive Child.

This chapter we will explore the Rebellious/Free Child State. It is often only called the Free Child or the Rebellious Child. For our purposes, I will call it both.

REBELLIOUS /FREE CHILD

NEGATIVE ATTRIBUTES	POSITIVE ATTRIBUTES
NO I WON'T!	ROCKS BOAT FOR CHANGE
ALL ABOUT ME!	NOT GUILT-DRIVEN
I DON'T CARE!	STANDS UP FOR SELF
VERY EMOTIONAL	HAS A VOICE!
OVERLY IMPULSIVE	CREATIVE
FEW BOUNDARIES	FREE-SPIRITED
TOO FREE SPIRITED	LIGHT-HEARTED
ACTION/NO FEAR OF	SPONTANEOUS
	OF CONSEQUENCES

The Rebellious/Free Child (R/FC) is one of the truly fun states to hang out in, if it's healthy. It's everything that is fun-loving and creative in your spirit. It's the side that is artistic and playful, energetic and adventurous. You know how we call teenagers *rebellious*? Well, this state celebrates everything about that time in our life: taking chances, finding our voice, finding our creative outlets, and having fun with no responsibility. I call it the ME STATE. It is also everything about us that is detrimental in both our teens and adulthood.

Positive Attributes

Let's first look at the positive traits of the Rebellious/Free Child. So many of the descriptions are all tied together in one concept: *action with no fear of consequences.* In order to be creative, we have to let go of all thoughts of boundaries, let go of the word "can't," or the fear of what others think. We need to take chances in order to be creative, to think outside the box. That's what creativity is. We are thinking outside of the known to create the unknown. It's an exciting, exhilarating, and adventurous endeavor. And those with a high or healthy R/FC state revel in it.

It is also what makes someone fun-loving and carefree. Think of the creative spirits you know and reflect on how much fun they are to be around. The R/FC taps into a side of the human spirit that almost screams EXCITING ENERGY! They don't worry about what others think. Unlike the critic, they are not being critical of themselves, so they can just BE. Unlike the nurturer, they are not tied up in others' needs, so they can experience their own needs. And for the R/FC, the need is being FREE: free of others' thoughts, expectations, and demands. That is why we see it as rebellion in teenagers. But rebellion is not a horrible thing.

When we talk about the R/FC's ability to think outside the box, we see that this is only possible when we stop worrying about others' opinions. History's greatest poets, scientists, artists, and writers are ones who took chances on their ideas and brought them to fruition. Many were heralded as brilliant in their day, and many were ostracized for breaking society's norms and rules. But they didn't care. Their R/FC was large enough to DO IT ANYWAY!

Another joyous and freeing side of the R/FC is the ability to be spontaneous, to not necessarily stick to expected behavior or routine ideas, but to jump to the unexpected! With an R/FC spirit, the rule is to *expect the unexpected*! R/FCs are not stopped by boundaries of any sort. If it's raining, they come up with something to do anyway. UNPLANNED OPPORTUNITIES is the way a R/FC sees any obstacle. The R/FC can throw out all rules and create a new experience. There is that word CREATE again!

The most glorious part of the R/FC is the VOICE that comes with it. A woman with a healthy Rebellious/Free Child state has found her own voice and is not afraid to use it. She is not worrying about the reactions of others and she speaks up. She may sometimes be right and sometimes wrong, but she does not keep her voice silent. She takes the chance to rebel and REVEAL herSELF to all who will listen, and to some who won't! Mostly she can show the world that she stands up for what she believes in. A healthy R/FC woman has no problem asking for her needs to be met. She has the healthy "it's okay to make this about ME" attitude. She does not shy away from her worth. She lives it, breathes it, and screams it.

In a healthy R/FC woman, guilt does not play a role in defining who she is. She does not do things out of guilt or because others decide that she should. She does things because they reflect who she is at the core of her being. Remember, it is the ME state. Her mantra is: "What makes ME HAPPY, what defines who I am?"

Are you any of these adjectives that work for an R/FC?

- Fun-loving
- Playful
- Spontaneous
- Artistic
- Creative
- Adventurous
- Outspoken
- Self-assured

Even if you only experience this occasionally in your day, check in to see if you honor your Rebellious/Free Child Spirit. Or even know it at all.

The Unhealthy Rebellious/Free Child

Now let's discuss the unhealthy traits of the Rebellious/Free Child. Now imagine a ME person who never looks at anyone else. Now SELFISHNESS rears its ugly head. One characteristic of the unhealthy R/FC is that ME never becomes WE. The first and foremost thought is always of themselves, rarely taking into consideration other people's wants or needs. Remember, the healthy nurturer weighs others' needs but includes her own needs in her final decision. The R/FC doesn't even SEE someone else's needs when she makes a decision. Or if she does, she ignores them. Frankly, with an R/FC, it is rarely a decision, but more often an impulse. "I don't care. I'll do it anyway."

Let's take the concept of making a DECISION a little further in regards to the R/FC. A decision means you have consciously looked at a situation and come to an understanding of what the final outcome should be, then acted on that decision. But unhealthy R/FC's often don't look at what the outcome of a decision could be.

They just act on impulse. They GO FOR IT without thinking about it! Spontaneity at its worst. This could be as simple as heeding the R/FC voice and blowing off work for the day or as intense as throwing their life away with over-indulgence, drugs, alcohol, gambling, or other rebellious addictions.

There is a huge danger in unhealthy Rebellious/Free Child spirits that happens when they act with no fear of consequences combined with spontaneity. It's called *denial.* They have to deny the possibility that there is a negative outcome to what they are doing so that they can continue with their rebellious behavior. And when they do that, they take away all of their boundaries. Boundaries are what the Critical Parent state sets to *protect us,* but high R/FC states throw boundaries on things, on people, and on themselves out the window. The rocky waters become a tidal wave.

For example, a healthy R/FC can have a drink to let loose and enjoy herself. She has a drink at a party, or at home to end the workday. She has a drink to enjoy a night out with the girls and relax. Then her Critical Parent side kicks in and sets a boundary to keep her safe. "One drink, or two max. I won't drive. Better eat something and stop now. *Ooh,* I need some water"—R/FC thoughts of the fun of alcohol WITH the CP BOUNDARIES. But when an unhealthy Rebellious/Free Child drinks with no fear of consequences, there is often no cut off, no boundaries. She often drinks till she is drunk and can no longer drive, is unsure of her actions, and truly doesn't care. This is R/FC gone bad. Sadly, excess often represents a level of freedom to certain people. They feel that they are their own boss, with no one telling them what to do. They have shut off their own Critical Parent voice, the voice that enforces boundaries. And they have revolted just like a teenager rebelling against her parents. And they have no guilt.

Yep. Just as a healthy R/FC has very little use for guilt, an unhealthy R/FC has NO GUILT. I often say to my clients that guilt has only one good reason: to look at something we want to change in our life. If we feel guilt, then it is a sign there is something we need to change. An unhealthy R/FC has no guilt because she does not choose to see that she needs to change anything about her rebellious self. Guilt would mean change is necessary, so she chooses to feel no guilt. It is the cycle of denial that breeds the most unhealthy R/FC characteristics. It is this denial that often rears its ugly head in extramarital affairs. This facet of a relationship always comes from the Rebellious/Free Child state. "It's all about me. I have no guilt. I don't care, and I have no desire to look at the consequences of my actions."

Another fascinating trait is when someone becomes TOO FREE-SPIRITED. It sounds harmless, right? After all, don't we crave being different sometimes? YES! I love a free-spirited person. I love someone who dresses the way they want to dress without caring what others think. I love people who make it okay to be different. But when someone becomes too free-spirited, they lose perspective on what's safe. For instance, a woman who sleeps with multiple partners with no use of protection. A woman who skips the beach alone, not caring that a man is following her. Or a woman who puts her child in danger because she wants to break all the rules. This is when free-spirited becomes reckless and logic goes out the window in favor of the adventurous or rule-breaking thinking of the Rebellious/Free Child state.

The trait that tops all of these unhealthy R/FC traits is that of becoming OVER-EMOTIONAL! Oh, yes. You have seen the teen who wants to be heard—DRAMA at its best! Well, this holds true for the unhealthy R/FC, too. When we say they have a VOICE, this is how they use it. They want to be heard and they will do everything to make that happen. This usually means becoming overly emotional, with tears, screaming, uncontrollable laughter, etc. Creative people often are more in touch with their emotional side. True. But when it comes to the unhealthy R/FC, they use emotion to gain attention or control a situation. Their emotion turns it from YOU to ME.

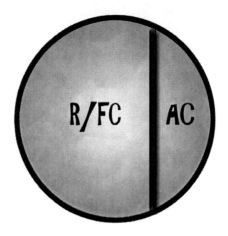

So where do you stand on the UNHEALTHY traits side of R/FC?

1. Do you go into denial and rebel in excess?
2. Have you lost your ability to look at others' needs and only concentrate on your own?
3. Have you lost friendships or relationships because of your unhealthy Rebellious/Free Child?
4. Has your work suffered from your Rebellious/Free Child behavior?
5. Is there some guilt you feel that you are denying in order to continue the behavior?
6. Do you use an overly emotional state to get your needs met?
7. Has your future suffered from avoiding good decisions?

The Missing Rebellious/Free Child

We have talked about an unhealthy Rebellious/Free Child and a healthy Rebellious/Creative Child, but there is another R/FC scenario in women that is very likely to walk in my office door—the "Missing Rebellious/Free Child." These are the people who have lost their creativity, spontaneity, playfulness, and the possibility of a ME state! It is not that rare nowadays. Work and money fears, child rearing, and lack of time have shut down many a R/FC spirit. Why?

Because in times of stress, people see the R/FC side as too frivolous or self-absorbed to acknowledge. They feel that their energy is better spent trying to drag themselves out of the muck with their other states. I won't disagree that we need all of the states to survive our challenges, but I wholeheartedly emphasize that the R/FC state has a lot to offer. And sometimes it is the same "rock the boat for change" that comes along to save us. Sometimes we need to "think outside the box" to give us a change in perception. More importantly, sometimes we need that Rebellious/Free Child state merely to give us a break from reality! Think about the words Free Child and Rebellious Child. Without that side of ourselves, we lose all spontaneity and joy in life. It is a prescription for the blues, for depression. So many women have practiced cutting off their R/FC to be "responsible" that they have lost their own voice. They hide their creativity and miss their own light-hearted soul.

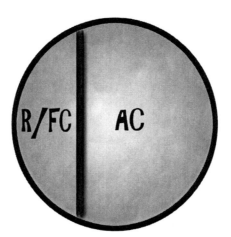

So, there is healthy R/FC, unhealthy R/FC, and no R/FC. Which are you? Can you draw the line and know when to end the fun? Do you use the tools of Rebellious/Free Child at the right times in your life? Are they hindering you or helping you? Do you have a creative side that is screaming to be released? Can you say, "Come on! Let's run out in the rain and play!"?

Chapter 8

The Adaptive Child State

ADAPTIVE CHILD

Negative Attributes	Positive Attributes
Helpless	Adaptable To Change
Submissive	Not Too Invested In Result
Seeks Approval	Trusting
Guilt Driven	Admits When Wrong
Never Gets Angry	Able To Ask For Help
Too Vulnerable	Able To Say I'm Sorry

You have just learned about one side of the child state, the Rebellious/Free Child. Now let's explore its counterpart, the Adaptive Child (AC). Where the Rebellious/Free Child is a ME state, the Adaptive Child is a YOU state—the sensitive, generous of spirit, kind, and vulnerable side of us all. It is similar to the Nurturing Parent in that it takes into account others' wishes and needs. It is a side that comes more naturally to women than to men, for many reasons. The Adaptive Child state means you really have to let go of control. Men are brought up believing that they need to be leaders, not followers. So for many people, their level of Adaptive Child is very gender-oriented. It is a very LEARNED or modeled state. Of course, that all depends on the parenting you received. For many women, it's a side that comes almost too easily, so they have to practice very hard not to be taken advantage of. For all of us, it is the softest side of our personality and the most flexible part of how we respond to everything from challenges to relationships. Hence the name ADAPTIVE CHILD.

Healthy Adaptive Child

One of the loveliest sides of the AC state is the way we use it to handle change, which is often extremely difficult for many people. It represents entering into the unknown. Just as the Rebellious/Free Child is a child state, the Adaptive Child state taps into the child-like spirit that lets us go with the flow. As a matter of fact, the person with a high AC is usually one of the easiest-going personalities to be around. Now I didn't say "fun." That is more the Rebellious/Free Child side. I said *easygoing*. The AC takes things in stride. The reason for this is the AC is not too invested in the outcome of a situation.

When we plan for something or have expectations that do not take place, a healthy person will call on their AC state to change their perception. A Critical Parent state will try to control the situation to get back to where they want it to be. A Rebellious/Free Child state will scream and yell till their needs are met, but an Adaptive Child personality will just say, "Okay, that option is out. What should we do now?" They are not EMOTIONALLY INVESTED in the outcome, so their mood is not affected by the end result. They are flexible and accommodating to a situation and to other people's needs.

One of the best tools that an AC has is the ability to ask for help. Now you see why I say men have a hard time with this state. It's the old joke that men can't ask for directions. The Adaptive Child state has very little ego. Remember, it's the YOU state. "I am so happy to have things be about you, not about me." This lovely part of AC is what keeps our ego out of the "asking for help" equation. It is the side of us that reaches outside of ourselves to get our needs met. Unlike the Nurturing Parent, where we are nurturing or helping others, AC is the state where we allow ourselves to ask for help; like the innocent small child in all of us, it's the part of us that is vulnerable and needs guidance or help. This side makes it okay to ask for help and the healthy Nurturing Parent is the side that makes it okay to receive help.

This brings to mind the concept of TRUST. If we are able to ask for help, that shows we trust someone else's guidance. Trust is truly one of the most beautiful and profound attributes of the healthy AC state. It is believing that we can make ourselves vulnerable with someone or something, both physically and emotionally, trusting that we will not be hurt. In relationships, it goes a step further and becomes our ability to share our deepest feelings and fears. We allow ourselves to let down our guard and let our mate into our hearts, our psyches, and our souls. WOW! That is pretty profound. Believe me, this is the hardest part for most women to understand: the idea that we need to learn to trust and become vulnerable, but not go overboard. Blind trust is not what makes a healthy AC. It's trust with a healthy dose of the *boundaries* of the Critical Parent. Trust itself is wholly an AC trait. Think once again of a child who trusts, until her parents teach her NOT to trust. The innocence of children is part of what we try to hold onto or bring back into our lives in order to have a gloriously healthy AC.

There is another tool that we learned as children that is representative of a healthy AC—the ability to say "I'M SORRY." Let's look at this for a minute. You hurt someone or do something wrong. The Rebellious/Free Child state says "so what," but the AC state is able to look beyond the ME and look at YOU, or at who or what they have wronged. First, it is the ability to look beyond ourselves to see where we may have hurt someone else. Then our AC State allows us to be vulnerable so we can find the space and voice to apologize. It is an extremely vulnerable place in a conflict to be able to apologize, which involves letting down your guard and not knowing if you will be hurt in return. You become egoless instead of ego-full. You reach out with open arms and ask for forgiveness. You don't know the outcome, but you do it anyway. Saying *I'm sorry* in relationships is one of the toughest things couples need to learn to do. Some people fear you are giving up your power when doing so. No, you are not giving up your power. You are trusting that by being true to your conscience and knowing you have wronged someone, you want to make it right. That is using your power in the most beautiful way for your own good. Regardless of the other person's reaction, you have done what is right. It is YOU who can be proud of YOU!

The Unhealthy Adapative Child

Now that we have looked at the healthy attributes of the Adaptive Child, let's look at the UNHEALTHY sides, the attributes that Adaptive Children manifest when they go overboard. The first, and one of the less harmful traits, is the overwhelming NEED FOR APPROVAL. When someone has this trait, they have lost their critical/critiquing abilities to see that the other person may be mistaken, may have chosen incorrectly, or is just plain wrong. They have also given up having a differing opinion, need, or desire. Rather than voicing their thoughts, they silence them in order to be accepted. We see this in teenagers who choose to be led by others. They are afraid to be different or not to join in for fear that they will not be accepted. Their overwhelming desire for acceptance overrides their own individual thoughts and choices. They want approval. When a woman grows up and holds onto this trait in her relationship, she ends up silencing her own voice for the acceptance and approval of her mate. Often it does not stop there. She silences her voice for the acceptance and approval of her friends, family, coworkers, and even strangers! It is a sign of low self-esteem. She is not honoring her own needs, but chooses to honor others. What's the *payoff*? BEING LIKED!

Another interesting trait of the unhealthy Adaptive Child is the way she uses guilt in her life to make her choices. I tell my clients that guilt is a useless emotion unless it is used to change something in our lives. "I feel guilty about something I am doing so I need to stop the behavior and change it." Or, "I feel guilty about something I have done in the past, or recent past, so I need to apologize for it." Once you have done that, then you need to forgive yourself and move on. There is no point in feeling guilty unless you have not addressed something you need to address. Once you address it and fix it, move on GUILT-FREE! That doesn't mean you may not have sadness, remorse, or other emotions around the event, but guilt should no longer be one of them. An unhealthy Adaptive Child, on the other hand, uses guilt as a motivator. Where an unhealthy Nurturing Parent uses guilt on others to smother them, the unhealthy Adaptive Child uses guilt on THEMSELVES. "I feel so guilty that I am going to punish myself by silencing my needs and making the world revolve around everyone else. I feel guilty allowing anything to be about me." Here is the tricky part: other people can sense this guilt-driven personality type, so when necessary, they use it to their advantage. In other words, when a man is in a relationship with a woman who can be manipulated by guilt, he uses it. Sadly, this is human nature. Actually, it is animal instinct. Survival of the fittest! Alpha dog! Guilt weakens us. It gives away our power, and someone who knows how to take advantage of that will.

I keep using the words NO VOICE or SILENCED. The most important concept behind these words is that the Adaptive Child is *not allowed to feel.* The unhealthy AC chooses not to feel her feelings because if she did, she would have to speak up! Instead she cuts off her feelings and stops acknowledging them. Especially anger. Unhealthy AC states NEVER show they are angry. After all, they would not be accepted. It would show how they are not adaptable. It would mean they were making something be about them! High AC people cut off their anger and never voice it. This leads me to the next more dangerous trait—HELPLESSNESS.

When the high AC cannot voice her emotions, she ends up helpless. She feels as if her voice has been taken away and she is helpless to get it back. This is often the case with people who have been either emotionally or physically abused. The safest reaction to the abusive high Critical Parent is to not speak, to shut down and shut off. The AC silences her voice for fear of the punishment that would accompany speaking up or defending herself. When you have no voice, you are afraid to ask for assistance, you are afraid to ask for protection, you are afraid to ask for anything. You cannot ask for help and you cannot help yourself. All the "thinking outside the box" of a Rebellious/Free Child is gone. The ME state disappears and the world has to revolve around the YOU, the abuser. So the AC sits in a place of helplessness. Remember earlier I said that defense mechanisms are needed to protect yourself against harm? Well, helplessness in this case is a defense mechanism that helps many AC people survive.

The problem for many women is that once the abuser is out of their lives, the AC continues to silence her voice. These women know nothing better than to take helplessness into all areas of their lives. At work, they are followers, not willing or feeling safe enough to lead. In relationships, they find very strong Critical Parent partners or very strong Rebellious/Free Child partners to balance out their helplessness. They cannot make decisions for themselves and they depend on others to do this for them. They feel SAFE this away and do not see it as weakness. Most likely, they do not see it at all. They only see that they do not have a voice to speak up and ask for their needs to be met. And this fits for them.

Not everyone has abuse in their background, yet they still have high unhealthy AC attributes. Let's talk about SUBMISSIVENESS. You can see where an abused person chooses to be submissive to survive, but this trait is not only practiced by abuse survivors, submissiveness is one of the many personality traits that women are taught is a *feminine* way to be. "Be submissive, be tolerant, be quiet, and let the man lead." We are modeled it, and we are told that it is the way to catch a man. By being submissive, we show the world that we want others to lead us. Whether it's a man, a boss, or a friend, those with high AC traits tend to feel more comfortable being submissive, giving in to others' wishes, and not ever asking for their needs to be met. Here is the scariest part: often they do not even have a thought of what their needs are! They are so programmed to not care that they don't even formulate their own wishes, dreams, or desires. Why would they? They are not going to ask for them anyway, so why bother having them? The clients that come to my office with highly submissive personalities are actually shocked when I offer them choices and tell them they can have what they desire.

We have mentioned how abuse is a precursor to the high AC state. Often, a female client is extremely submissive if she comes from a foreign country that has strict patriarchal beliefs—beliefs that a man is in control and a woman should not speak up. I also see this in second-generation American women from the same kinds of cultures. This is also prevalent in American women who come from certain religious backgrounds where women have no voice. Remember, we are programmed as children, so if we are programmed to be adaptive to men, we tend to choose men that we can be adaptive to. It is rare to see a very strong woman with a high Adaptive Child state in a relationship with another high AC person. They could not exist together very long. This is why we say opposites attract! I see this often with clients who have married a man from a highly patriarchal culture. When I dig, I find out that their upbringing told them THEY HAVE NO VOICE. Whether it was abuse, religion, or even a mother who tried to keep them silenced, they have acquired all of the most painful attributes of the AC, the attributes that confirm that they don't exist.

Case in point. I have a client who was extremely abused by her ex-husband. She made the only choice she could to stay in a marriage that she was too afraid to leave. She chose to GIVE UP any thought of self. When it came to restaurants, it was where he wanted to go. When it came to where they would live, she let him decide. When it came to the way he treated their children, it was always his way. When it came to how she did her hair or nails or dressed, it was what made him happy. To avoid abuse, conflict, and stress, she gave up any personal choice, desire, or dream of her own. She shut down any ability she had to CHOOSE and basically decided to decide nothing. SHE HAD NO VOICE. She was a hugely unhealthy Adaptive Child married to a hugely unhealthy Critical Parent.

When someone becomes a completely unhealthy Adaptive Child, the psyche handles it with depression. Giving up your soul for someone else can only lead to depression. Then with depression come so many unhealthy tools to survive it: drugs, alcohol, self-abuse. You are so used to being abused, that you abuse yourself. This is what usually happens with a hugely unhappy and unhealthy Adaptive Child who has lost all the rebellion needed to stand up for herself. She has lost all of her ME state. The only way she can rebel is by self-medicating. In teenagers who have a very controlling parent in their life, they often turn to eating disorders, as food intake is the only thing in their life they can control.

As a therapist, I can only hope that when this happens, someone in their life steps in to save them. Sometimes it's a parent, or friend, or child. And sometimes it's the law. Whatever it is, something or someone shows them that they deserve happiness and their needs deserve to be acknowledged. Then it is their Adaptive Child's ability to ask for help that starts them on a path to healing.

Your Adaptive Child State

So let's check in with your ADAPTIVE CHILD state. Is it healthy? Is it unhealthy? Is it even there?

Ask yourself:

1. Are you able to say you're sorry?
2. Do you tell people you are sorry even when you know you did nothing wrong?
3. Do you keep your emotions hidden for fear of someone else's reaction?
4. Do you speak up for your own needs?
5. Are you more comfortable as a follower than as a leader?
6. Are you missing out in life because you won't speak up for yourself?
7. Do you change parts of your life to be accepted by others?
8. Are you adaptable to change?
9. Does change frustrate you?
10. Do you get angry?

11. Does it bother you if someone does not like you?

Remember we *need* this state, but we need it healthy. Yes, there are times when we say we are sorry. Yes, there are times when it feels wonderful to accommodate other's needs. Yes, sometimes we need to hold in our emotions, but not when it is a detriment to our own soul!

Now look at your Child states circle. Are you a bigger Rebellious/Free Child with a small Adaptive Child state? Are you a bigger Adaptive Child with a smaller Rebellious/Free Child state? Or are you a healthy balanced woman with a healthy, even, child state—sometimes rebellious, sometimes adaptive—and you choose the right state at the right time?

Chapter 9

The Adult State

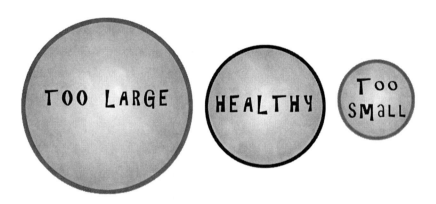

ADULT

NEGATIVE ATTRIBUTES	POSITIVE ATTRIBUTES
I'M THINKING	OBJECTIVE
TOO ANALYTICAL	GOOD ON THE JOB
TOO UNEMOTIONAL	BALANCED DECISION-MAKING
NOT SPONTANEOUS	BALANCED EMOTIONS
DECISIONS BASED ON LOGIC	USES LOGIC TO
	ADVANTAGE,
OR POOR DECISION-MAKING	NOT FEELINGS
IMBALANCED EMOTIONS	
COMPLETELY ILLOGICAL	
TOO SUBJECTIVE	

WELCOME TO THE LAST chapter on the five sides to YOU. This one is about the ADULT state. As I shared with you in chapter 4, the ADULT state is whole unto itself. It doesn't have an antithesis. It *does* have healthy and unhealthy traits, so when it is imbalanced, it is either too big or too small.

The Healthy Adult State

The most fascinating part of a healthy adult state is that it is based on making decisions without letting emotions play a part. It is the ability to make a decision logically, based on facts. LOGICAL! FACTS! Many of you would say that is impossible as we are humans, not robots. You are right. So let's say that we DO have emotions around a decision, the goal in using our Adult state is first to separate out our emotions from the facts and, second, to make a healthy decision. This, ladies, is the purpose of this state: LOGICAL, UNEMOTIONAL DECISION-MAKING.

Emotions can sometimes skew our judgment to the point where we lose track of the facts. Being human and being women, we tend to lead with our emotions. For many, emotions often build on themselves until we lose all sight of the logic in a situation. The famous saying that "emotion carried me away" is why we need a healthy Adult state so we can sift through our emotions and be guided to the best answer or best course of action. The beauty of using this state is it also brings us PEACE! When we can separate our emotions from our logical thinking, we can breathe easier, think more clearly, and inevitably feel calmer and more peaceful as we navigate the challenges and choices in our lives.

The Adult state is *objective*, which means you are making choices that are not influenced by your opinions. Okay, how hard is THAT? We all have opinions. But, when we are coming from our most Adult state, our opinions are left out of the equation. We are simply weighing the facts to bring us to a conclusion.

Let's take a look at when this can be to our advantage. WORK! Having a healthy ADULT state helps us on the job. When we can separate out illogical thinking and stick to reality, we can accomplish so much more and do it faster! Practicing your Adult state at work shows your associates, bosses, and employees that you can be counted on to make healthy decisions based on logic. It creates a level of safety in the work environment that means others can rely on you to communicate and react from a logical place and not from a self-absorbed or emotional place. When you can keep your Rebellious/Free Child or Critical Parent in check, you get a level of respect from everyone around you. The Rebellious/Free Child traits of creativity and thinking outside the box are great attributes for an employee, but only when they are tempered by a healthy Adult state that lets you know when it is appropriate to use them. Critical thinking is often needed when setting boundaries at work, or for managing employees, but again, tempered by the logical checks and balances of the Adult state and, most importantly, communicated through the Adult state.

So when is the Adult state unhealthy? When your Adult state is either TOO BIG or TOO SMALL. Let's start with too small, which is often associated with women.

Too Small Adult State

"Women are so emotional." Okay, that's partly true. Women tend to be more in touch with their emotions than men are. We were given this right from childhood. Society said that it was okay to feel hurt and express our emotions, though your own upbringing may not have allowed it. In general, it was expected that women were MORE emotional then men. Men were taught to stuff their emotions down. Well, shouldn't that mean that they would have a very healthy Adult unemotional state? Actually, NO! Just because they buried their emotions does not mean that they do not have them or that they can keep their hidden emotions from entering into their decision-making process. So when we talk about the Adult state, this makes us equals. We ALL have to find a healthy Adult state, whether our emotions are hidden or sitting right on the surface for the entire world to see. Male or female, we need to learn to balance decisions with logic.

When men or women have too small of an Adult state, they let their emotions influence, guide, or rule them to the point where they have weakened or poor decision-making tools. They cannot separate fact from fiction. The too small Adult state person often does not have *any* level of logic in their thought process, communication skills, and relationships. They see things from a totally SUBJECTIVE perspective instead of an OBJECTIVE perspective. It is all based on gut feelings, or sadly, on bad emotional defense mechanisms. You know that kind of person—the one who cannot stay centered long enough to discuss something rationally. The one who throws illogical thinking at you when you try to discuss the facts. The worst part is that kind of person can drag you out of your own logical state into a place of total psychosis, where you just want to scream! When you are dealing with someone who has a very small Adult state, you have to work really hard to remain peaceful and have an adult conversation. Yep, there it is: ADULT! They are so good at their illogical thinking that they can even get you to question what you know are *facts*. This is just one outcome for a small Adult state. *Hmm*, is that you?

Logical thinking

When is it okay to use your emotions? Let me make clear that I am not turning you into unemotional robots. Often we do base decisions on emotions, passion, instinct, or intuition. The difference between that and the above scenario is that you are *aware* you are basing your thinking on emotions versus being *ruled* by your emotions. That's a big difference! It's a choice rather than a reaction. And that, lovely ladies, in itself is LOGICAL thinking. You have weighed your logical thinking with your emotional instincts and gone with your emotions.

For example, you need to decide whether or not to take a certain job. Logical thinking tells you that the pay is great, the environment is healthy, the drive is easy, and the job suits you. Yet you have this nagging feeling that you should NOT take the job. Call it women's intuition or a gut feeling. Whatever it is, it is saying STOP. Emotion! If you are using a healthy adult state, you will look at all the facts, including your gut feeling as a fact. Then decide. When you do this, you are honoring all sides of you and not letting one or the other rule you. THAT is a healthy Adult state.

Now let's say the same situation is in front of you except you have three kids to feed and you have been out of work for months. The wolf is at the door! Hopefully, when you weigh THOSE facts, logic will win over the emotion. You will take the job.

Too Large Adult State

Next let's look at the TOO LARGE Adult state. I call this the "get a life syndrome." The person with too large of an Adult state is so logical in their thinking that there is no space or time for the fun, spontaneity, and vulnerability of life. You can see that those three words all demand emotions. So when life revolves solely around logical decisions, then humanity cannot come into play. Spirit and heart cannot come into play. It's the Get A Life Syndrome. Remember, a healthy Adult state is *not* about not having emotions; it is about knowing when and where to let emotions affect your choices. It is learning to listen to your emotions, acknowledge them, and then balance them with logic. Those with too large an Adult state choose not to acknowledge their feelings at all. Often, they are so squelched that they do not even know the emotions are there. Sadly, the person with a too large Adult state often cannot acknowledge someone else's emotions or needs, especially if it affects his or her logical decision. These people are often labeled as cold-hearted.

For example, I had a family in my office with a father who truly was a HUGE Adult state—very emotionally closed off. Everything was checks and balances. Decisions about the kids rarely involved fun. His marriage was so logical that the romance had disappeared. It was so bad that when they did finally schedule a vacation, at my insistence, he planned each part of it down to the minute. All decisions as to where to go and what to do were based on logical reasons. "If we go to this town, Joey can also look at a college. If we eat at this restaurant, it will be exactly halfway to the next town." He even scheduled the bathroom stops on the trip! According to him, there would be no changes. The GET A LIFE SYNDROME!

Many of you will look at your Adult state and realize that it is perfectly healthy at work, but not in your personal life. It's easier to use your Adult state in your workplace or for your outside commitments than to use it in your personal life. That makes sense. Our personal life should be filled with feelings, instincts, emotions, heart and soul. It is human spirit. You need to be able to draw from all five states to have a healthy relationship with others and with yourself. But just as important as the other four states are in your personal life, so is the Adult state. It may not be as easy, but it is just as important.

An interesting point to look at when you examine your own Adult state is recognizing who you feel safe to be logical with, who triggers your emotions, who causes you to lose your logic, and with whom do you HAVE to be the logical one because he or she is not.

Your Adult State

Let's check in with your Adult state. Is it healthy? Unhealthy? Is it too big or too small? Do you use it at work? Do you use it in your personal world?

1. At work, do you make decisions based on logic or emotions?
2. Do you deal with work challenges from a logical fact-solving place or an emotional place?
3. Do you deal with personal challenges from a logical fact-solving place or an emotional place?
4. At home with family, mates, kids, neighbors, parents, do you let logic help balance your decisions or do you lead with emotions?

5. In a crisis, do you react emotionally first and then make decisions? Or do you react logically to solve the crisis?
6. Do you have to calm yourself down to make a decision?
7. Do people ever tell you that you are too cold-hearted?
8. Do people ever tell you that you are too emotional?
9. Name the people you feel safe being logical with.
10. Name the people who trigger your emotions and less logical self.
11. Name the people that you HAVE to be logical with because they are not.
12. Was your Mom logical, balanced, or emotional?
13. Was your Dad logical, balanced, or emotional?
14. What about your mate?
15. How about your best friend?

The Adult state is like the roots for our healthy psychological brain. If this state is strong and nourished, it will keep the checks and balances of the other states healthy. It will keep the Parent state balanced between Nurturing Parent and Critical Parent by judging which is the healthier state to use at the time. It will keep the Child state balanced by quieting the unhealthy voice and strengthening the healthy one. It is for this reason that the Adult State is seen as a whole circle with no other half. You either have it or you don't. It is either a small Adult State, a healthy size, or too big. Adult state is just that—the adult side of our personality, the side that helps us grow into the healthiest adults we can be. Not a parent, not a child . . . an Adult.

Now you have learned about the five sides to your personality. Hopefully, you have used your healthy Critical Parent voice to look at yourself. Hopefully, you have balanced out that voice with facts, via your Adult voice. Hopefully, you have nurtured yourself through these chapters with your Nurturing Parent voice as you head towards self-awareness. Hopefully, you have thought outside the box with your Rebellious/Free Child voice to come up with new ways to think and feel. And hopefully, your Adaptive Child voice is helping you feel the desire to adapt and change to become a healthier, happier, and much more aware human being.

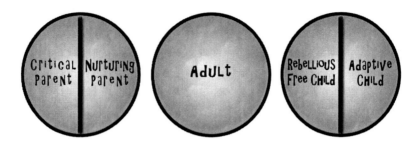

Chapter 10

Me

LADIES, WHAT GREAT WORK you have done so far! You have dug in and started the search for self-awareness. I am hoping over the course of this book that you have had many *AHA* moments! My guess is that you have not only critiqued yourself, but have also critiqued half of your relationships, family, and friends! In this chapter we will put it all together and see what your personality chart looks like. We will look at the healthy states and the imbalanced states. We will touch on how you became this person and then we are going to talk about how to change into the happiest, healthiest woman you can be.

To start, look at this graph below. This is what THE HEALTHY FIVE SIDES of our personality should look like.

The Parent state is balanced equally between the Critical Parent and the Nurturing Parent. The Child state is balanced equally between the Rebellious/Free Child and the Adaptive Child state. Then right in the middle you have a whole healthy Adult state. This chart is what we all aspire to be! Don't worry, few of us are actually this healthy. Hopefully, with more and more self-evaluation and self-awareness, you will get there, or pretty darn close!

Now it's your turn. Look at the blank circle below and first draw a line in the Parent state, splitting it to show the size of your Nurturing Parent versus the size of your Critical Parent.

It could look something like any of these samples.

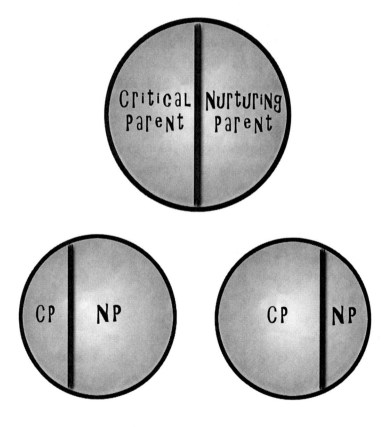

Now look at the blank circle below and draw the line showing the size of your Rebellious/Free Child versus your Adaptive Child.

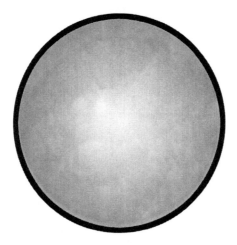

It could look like any of these samples.

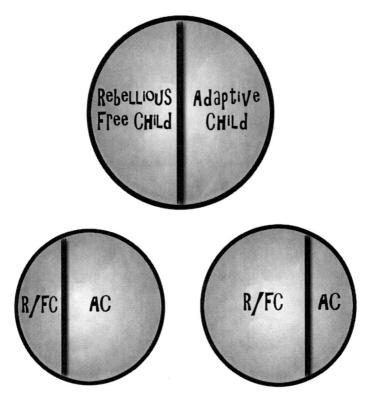

Now it is time to chart your ADULT state. You need to see if your Adult state is either too large, too small, or perfect. If the below circle is Healthy, draw inside it or outside of it the size of your Adult State.

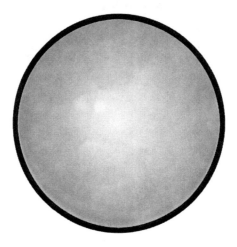

It could look like any of these.

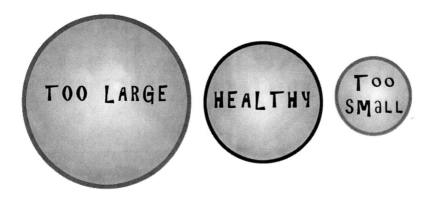

Now transfer them all over to this blank chart. PARENT, ADULT, CHILD

WOW! HERE YOU ARE ON PAPER! What do you look like? Are there things that you have learned about your balance or imbalance that come as a surprise to you? Or maybe you have you always *felt* like this but never had a way to make sense of all these emotions and behaviors, thoughts and defense mechanisms. Now that you have looked at YOU, evaluated YOU, and started to LOVE the YOU that has been discovered, next we will look at *how* you came to be who you are. YOUR PARENTS! Ready? Here we go!

Your Parents

Remember way back at the beginning of this book I told you that we are like computers that have been programmed by our parents, teachers, brothers and sisters? I want you to quickly chart out what your parents, or major caretakers, were like. (LOL, as if you hadn't done that already.)

CHART DAD

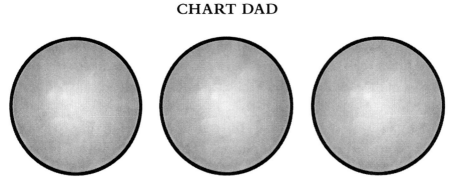

CHART MOM

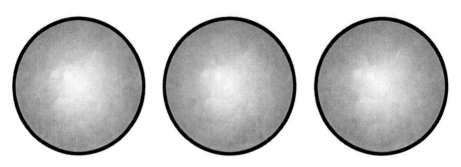

Now let's think about how growing up with these charts as parents affected your life. Here are just a few scenarios for each of the different states. I cannot go through all of the different mixes and matches since that would be a book in itself, but I will touch on the most typical. See where you may fit.

CRITCAL PARENT = Adaptive Child

Did you have one or both parents with a very large Critical Parent state? If so, there is a huge chance that you became the Adaptive Child. The pleaser. Remember, the one with no voice? The confusing part here is that as children we are supposed to obey our parents. So there are definitely Adaptive traits that are healthy while we grow up. This is the state that is malleable, willing and able to adapt your needs to fit others. But when you have an overly Critical Parent, you are taught that you have no voice or that your voice doesn't matter. You are often emotionally, and sometimes physically, beaten down to total submission. So the best way for a child to grow up in this environment is to become the pleaser. You choose to keep the peace at all costs by never having an opinion that interferes with those of the Critical Parent. You learn how to disregard any personal needs to make sure that only the Critical Parent's needs are satisfied. Many adaptive children have gotten so good at being Adaptive that they don't feel repressed or unhappy. They actually feel safer being Adaptive than being any other state. Until they grow up. Note that having a healthy Critical Parent is one of the true blessings in life.

They teach you healthy boundaries, protect you, guide you, and teach you to have strong morals, ethics, and values. It is only when they are unhealthy that you become an Adaptive Child in order to survive.

CRITICAL PARENT = Rebellious/Free Child

The other typical response to having a Critical Parent in your life is to become the Rebellious/Free Child. This kind of child who won't allow herself to be bullied or criticized without a really good fight. You are truly the opposite of the NO VOICE Adaptive Child; you have a *huge* voice and demand to be heard. Or you demand to be allowed to be your *own* Critical Parent, setting your own rules, deciding what you want and making sure the Critical Parent hears it. This is by no means a safe choice. It is often a very bold personality with a huge survival mechanism that chooses this route because it is absolutely the toughest way to live with a Critical Parent.

NURTURING PARENT = Nurturing Parent

Did you have a very Nurturing Parent who taught you that nurturing was the right way to be in life, so you became ruled by your OWN Nurturing Parent state? Nurturers often breed nurturers, especially women. Women tend to have a more nurturing spirit in the first place as the result of thousands of years of multi-generational learning and modeling. If you were modeled that a woman needs to be nurturing, there is a good chance you grasped onto this state very easily. Just remember that if it is healthy, it's wonderful. But if it is unhealthy, you often nurture everyone but yourself.

NURTURING = Rebellious/Free Child or Critical Parent

If you have an overly Nurturing Parent, there is a huge chance that you were trained right into the ME state of the Rebellious/Free Child. Your parent did the nurturing to such a huge degree that you never had to give back. You got to make the world all about you. The probability is that the *power* in this state also bred some Critical Parent traits. When a child is given too much power without boundaries, they often turn into a Critical Parent with a huge Rebellious Child side.

REBELLIOUS/ FREE CHILD = Nurturing Parent or Adult state

Often when you have a Free Child for a parent, life is full of fun and excitement. Music or the arts may be rampant in your life. When it is healthy, the R/FC parent creates a child with a healthy Free Child spirit—spontaneous, fun loving, and playful. But when it goes overboard into Rebellion, it is often a parent with a drug or alcohol problem. In this case, the child becomes the Adult because someone has to be logical. Or they become the Nurturer. Again there needs to be someone to take care of the "adult" Rebellious/Free Child. We call this being "parentified." When the parents act like kids to an unhealthy extreme, the kids tend to become the parents in the household, or the ones acting like the adult or the nurturer. I once had a seven-year-old boy who was living with his alcoholic mother. At seven years old, he was the one making the meals and the only one taking care of himself.

REBELLIOUS/FREE CHILD = Adaptive Child

Another typical scenario are the Rebellious/Free Child parents who make the whole world about THEM. Did you have a huge Rebellious/Free Child parent that made the world all about him or her, forcing you into being the Adaptive one? Were they so rebellious that they never even acknowledged others and expected you to give in? Did you have the parent that was SO BIG that you had to stay SMALL in life? Becoming an Adaptive Child to a parent who is a strong Rebellious/Free Child seems like an easy way to endure the lifestyle of a Rebellious Parent. But in truth it harbors much sadness, as you are basically made to believe you don't exist.

These are just some examples of how UNHEALTHY parents create the people we turn into. And these are extremes! Everyone has different variations of healthy and unhealthy. Hopefully you had parents with some truly balanced personality states that helped mold you into a balanced, happy child-turned-adult. It is fascinating to think of the many scenarios that could have helped create the woman you are today.

Now that I have described the myriad of recipes that could have created YOU, take a look at the charts of your caretakers/parents and see if you can figure out how their personality charts affected who you grew up to be.

Siblings

Next you can chart your siblings to see what their charts look like compared to yours. When you start to do this kind of charting, you will begin to see the patterns in your family. You will see why your siblings are the way they are. You will see how not only your parents but also your siblings molded your personality. For instance, if you have one sibling who is very nurturing, he or she may allow you to be the more powerful critical one, or you may become the Rebellious Child. If you have one sibling who is very rebellious, you may become the Adaptive Child. Or you could become the Adult, trying to keep them in check! There are so many ways that we co-create our family dynamic. By investigating your family's personality charts, you can see what you chose and why you chose it.

Who do you want to be?

The question then becomes: Is the person you became in your family dynamic the one you want to be as an adult? Where do you recreate these patterns? In your work? In your friendships? In relationships? Most importantly, now that you are *aware* of these states, is it helping your life or hurting YOU? Are you genuinely healthy?

Is it nurture or nature? Were you born with these traits—adaptive, rebellious, nurturing, critical, logical? Were you always destined to be the shy one or the boisterous one? Or could your personality all be defense mechanisms created so you could *fit into* your family system? Remember I said that defense mechanisms are choices that we make to help us defend ourselves against harm. Let's think about that for a minute. Your nature may have been to be a fun-loving child. But if you had a very Critical Parent who wanted to tame you, he or she first tried to program the fun-loving side out of you. If that didn't work, he or she overused the Critical Parent side to bully you to create the person he or she wanted you to be. Eventually, to defend yourself against the harm caused by an abusive parent or an overly Critical Parent, you choose to protect yourself by becoming an Adaptive Child—giving in. Both the programming by your parent and your use of defense mechanisms to protect yourself caused you to lose your Rebellious/Free Child spirit.

Take some time with this chapter and what it means before you move on to the next one. This is very intense work and may bring up old issues about your past and your family. Or it may bring up new issues about who you are today. I want you to be gentle with yourself. I want you to remember that this is a journey. I want you to nurture yourself through the journey as you use your Critical Parent and Adult state to evaluate your chart. But use your healthy critical CRITIQUING side, not your judgmental side. Then I want you to use your Nurturing Parent state to soothe you on your path to self-awareness.

As Sally Field has said, *"I have only watched my feet as I've moved through life and am amazed to see the distance I have traveled."*

Chapter 11

You, Me, And The Horse
You Rode In On

WELCOME BACK. I HOPE you really took some time with the last chapter to do some research on your chart, your family's charts, and your journey to self-awareness. Why? Because now we are going to look at how your programming has affected the relationships in your life.

This is the crux of this book: since we were conditioned to become the people we are in our charts, if we don't work to balance out our unhealthy states, then we will find a mate who allows us to stay in the role we are most comfortable in. Healthy or not healthy, we will recreate the same dynamics in our relationships that worked in our family dynamic.

Here are some examples:

If we are the adaptive one in our family, the pleaser, the one who does not speak up, then we find a man who is critical and controlling, or rebellious, so that we can continue in the role we are so comfortable in, the Adaptive Child. On the other side of the unhealthy chart, if we are the critical one, then we will find an adaptive person who allows us to be in control. Why? Because it is with them that we are most comfortable to be our unhealthy selves. Now you can understand the concept behind the old belief that opposites attract. But here is the truth: if you are not healthy and he is not healthy, and it is just two people filling in the voids in their own chart, then disaster is imminent for the relationship.

So guess where I am going now? Right! Next you are going to chart your past lovers or mates and see what their charts look like compared to yours.

CHART OF YOUR LAST LOVER

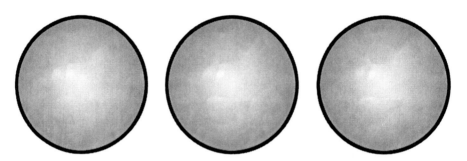

Did you search out a man who is the opposite of you? How did that work for you? Did you find a healthy balanced mate, yet you were not healthy? Did you repeat your family pattern in your love life? Is your ex's chart just like your dad's or your mom's?

Next I want you to take a look at the "history" of your relationships. As we are constantly growing, healing human beings, there is the hope that after each relationship we learn more about what is good for us and what is not. So I want you to go into your past and chart the last *few* relationships and what YOUR chart looked like within those relationships. What you are looking for is the pattern of men you have chosen and your pattern of behavior with them.

THEIR CHART - MY CHART

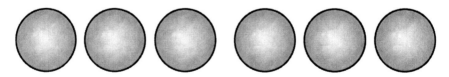

THEIR CHART - MY CHART

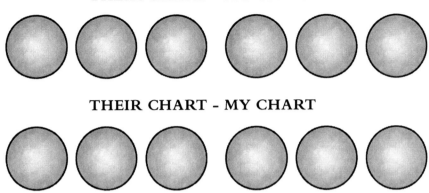

THEIR CHART - MY CHART

Examine these charts very closely. See if there was a pattern of growth as you went from one to the next. I want you to become aware of whether you changed and learned from each one, or if you think you have repeated the same unhealthy relationships over and over again.

There is an interesting phenomenon that often takes place as we go from one relationship to the next. Sometimes after you break free of an unhealthy relationship, you actually rebel and become the OPPOSITE of the person you were in that relationship. I call it the "pendulum swing." Often Adaptive people rebel and go hog wild Rebellious! Or Nurturers decide the hell with it and become frustrated critics, giving back in the new relationship what they hated in their past relationship. Look at your patterns. Are you one of these people? If so, IT'S OKAY! Sometimes we have to practice a state we have never been in before in order to figure it out. Or we have to at least experience it. How many women do you know who were quiet stay-at-home moms, and then once they got divorced they turned into WILD WOMEN? They are practicing a side that has been dormant for way too long. It's like a coke bottle that has been shaken up and then finally the top comes off!

Here is something to think about, in the words of a great poet: *"Two halves have little choice but to join; and yes, they do make a whole. But two wholes, when they coincide, that is beauty. That is love."* Peter McWilliams (1970).

Chapter 12

How Do I Change?

WELCOME TO YOUR WORLD. You have just done some very intense work on your journey to self-awareness. Often when you learn so much about your own conditioning, you feel like a character whose life was written by your parents. Sometimes, even as an adult, you feel you are still playing a role that someone else created for you. Or it may feel like you understand yourself and your choices for the very first time. It could also be a crazy combination of both. What I want you to know is that *who you are today* does not have to stay the same. You now have at your fingertips the tools to balance your personality chart so you can become the woman YOU want to be. We have a great saying in therapy: "When you make the subconscious conscious, it can go away." You probably have already become highly aware of your imbalances from reading these chapters. Hopefully, you have started to take tiny steps to balance out the imbalances. But what I am going to do next is give you a PLAN OF ACTION for becoming self-aware. Are you ready? Here goes!

Action Plan to Balance My Life

1. THE STATE OF THE WEEK—SELF-AWARENESS
2. JOURNALING QUESTIONNAIRE—WILLINGNESS
3. CHANGE—ACTION

For the next five weeks you will be doing your own therapy! That's right. You will be your own investigator, guide, and healer.

Each week you are going to choose ONE of the five personality states—CP, NP, R/FC, AC, or A—to work on. You are going to immerse yourself in the self-awareness of that state. You are going to learn if you rule it or it rules you!

THE STATE OF THE WEEK—SELF-AWARENESS

1. Pick a state to practice for a week. Make a list of the positive and negative traits of that state and keep it with you at all times to refer to over the course of the week.

2. Become completely aware of *every time* you make a decision from that state, communicate from that state, or behave like that state. This makes you be completely self-aware for the entire week.

3. Look at the traits and see if your behavior was on the positive traits side or the negative traits side. Did you react in a healthy or unhealthy way? Did you make decisions out of old habits or because you made a conscious choice about how you wanted to act, think, and behave?

4. If you find yourself back to non–awareness and forget to evaluate yourself as the day goes on, then recap your behavior and thoughts at the end of the day and see if you can tell when and where you reacted from the state of the week.

5. Towards the end of the seven days, OVER-PRACTICE this state's healthy side. So, if you never have fun and you are on the Rebellious/Free Child state, make it a point to have fun! You will find that you need to over-practice the states in order to find the balance.

6. At the end of the week, journal what the week has taught you about your life-long programming and how you want to be today.

DO THIS EXERCISE EVERY WEEK FOR FIVE WEEKS UNTIL YOU HAVE LIVED AND BREATHED AND KNOWN EACH OF THESE STATES AND HOW THEY AFFECT

YOUR PERSONALITY, EMOTIONS, COMMUNICATION, RELATIONSHIPS AND, MOST IMPORTANTLY, YOUR LIFE CHOICES. Do it for an entire week because chances are that you will find yourself in many different life scenarios and exposed to many different relationships over the course of a week. If you cheat and only do it for a day or a few days, you may not learn as much about yourself.

JOURNALING QUESTIONNAIRE—WILLINGNESS

After you have done the exercise in self-awareness for five weeks, take a look at what changing yourself, balancing yourself, and knowing yourself mean to you. We need to do a litmus test of your WILLINGNESS to change. Sometimes we have to know how change is going to help us, or how *not* changing will hurt us. So journal and answer the below questions. The beauty of these questions is that you can use them and make changes this month. Then use them over the next months until you are living the profoundly healthy and genuine life you dream of. Self-aware!

1. Have you been aware of the imbalances in your chart, or are they new to you?
2. Have you known they are there, but you've been in denial about how they are affecting your life?
3. Do an inventory of how your imbalances have negatively affected your life.
4. Have you chosen people in your life who continue to feed your imbalances?
5. Have you chosen jobs or circumstances that feed your imbalances?
6. Do you really want to change?
7. What are the payoffs for staying in your dysfunctional or imbalanced state?
8. Are you afraid of giving up sides of yourself that you identify with? These can be labels, or characteristics like pleaser, rebel, boss, leader, helper, healer, nice guy, etc.

9. Are you willing to let go of certain identity traits and to replace them with new ones?

10. Are you afraid of other people's reactions if you start voicing sides of you that have been dormant, or stop sharing sides of you that they are used to seeing?

11. Are there certain people with whom you feel safe while you are changing and growing?

12. Are there certain people who will try to manipulate you back to the old you?

13. Are you afraid of damaging or losing certain relationships by changing into a healthier person?

14. Are you afraid of practicing a state that may release old demons and cause you to lose control?

15. How much are you willing to change about yourself?

16. How will you feel about yourself if you don't at least TRY to change?

17.

The last step in this journey to BALANCE is to make some decisions and take action to change. It is a whole chapter in itself.

Chapter 13

Change—Action

WELCOME TO THE HARDEST chapter in the book. Change! Until now you have learned about yourself, dissected yourself, loved yourself, and judged yourself. Hopefully, the last chapter has brought some self-awareness as to WHY you want to change. Next I am hoping that you are ready to look at HOW you want to change. In this chapter we are going to take one state at a time and gently look at WHAT you are *willing to change*. The real work of self-awareness and change is a lifelong process. I tell my clients that finding their healthiest genuine self is like peeling an onion. You start with one layer, peel it, and see what is below. Then after you live with that layer for a while, you peel it and find a whole new layer. Self-awareness is a lifetime of learning, changing, and growing.

Below is a list of questions for you to answer in your journal. While doing this, think of your relationships with lovers, family, and friends and, most importantly, your relationship with yourself. You will answer the same questions for each state. Remember, balancing some states means practicing them MORE, while balancing other states mean practicing them LESS. It also means practicing the POSITIVE attributes of the state and getting rid of the NEGATIVE attributes. Go through each of these states, one by one, with gentleness and willingness. Honor yourself through this work. Be proud of any step you choose towards happiness and health!

When you answer the questions, think of how you communicate, the words you use, the morals, ethics, or values you have chosen, the people in your life, jobs you have had, how you treat others, how you treat yourself, self-talk, habits that you have acquired, belief systems you have embraced, and on and on and on. Consider these questions to be your very own yellow brick road to *your* OZ. Remember, it is only a start. Now get ready, click your heels three times, and let's go!

CRITICAL PARENT

Negative Attributes	Positive Attributes
Negative	Protector
Controlling	Sets Boundaries
Opinionated	Enforces Values
Confrontational	Sense Of Power
Critical	Good Critic

What are three small things you can change to balance your Critical Parent state?

1.

2.

3.

What are three bigger things you would like to WORK ON CHANGING about your Critical Parent state?

1.

2.

3.

Journal Questions:
- How will changing these things make you feel about yourself?
- In what way will making these changes have an impact on your life?

- What is some attribute you have that you are not ready to change right now?
- What is stopping you?
- What will it take to start making that change?
- How will starting it change your life?
- What attributes of this state do you have that you are proud to own?
- How have those attributes helped your life?
- Where do you think you learned them?
- How has *not* having a balanced Critical Parent state hurt your life?
- How will balancing your Critical Parent state change your life?

Now that you have evaluated your Critical Parent, here are a few simple HINTS ON HOW TO BALANCE YOUR CRITICAL PARENT.

<u>If your CP is too high</u>:
- Stop judging yourself and others.
- LET GO of control!
- Love yourself more, love others more.
- Practice tolerance.
- Listen to all your negative self-talk about yourself and others.
- Learn how to filter your criticisms, or balance them with logic.
- CHOOSE LOGIC over criticism as much as possible.

<u>If your CP is too low</u>:
- Be a healthier critic of people, places, and things.
- Set stronger boundaries.
- Practice taking back your control.
- Try to define your own morals, ethics, and values versus letting others do it for you.
- Find tools that help you stand up and protect yourself.

NURTURING PARENT

NEGATIVE ATTRIBUTES	POSITIVE ATTRIBUTES
S/MOTHERING	FEEL NEEDED
OTHERS NOT SELF	SELF-CARE
SELF-CARE IS SELFISH	HEALING
BLINDED TO OTHERS FAULTS	SELFLESS GIVING

What are three small things you can change to balance your Nurturing Parent state?

1.

2.

3.

What are three bigger things you would like to WORK ON CHANGING about your Nurturing Parent state?

1.

2.

3.

Journal Questions:
- How will changing these things make you feel about yourself?
- In what way will making these changes have an impact on your life?
- What is some attribute you have that you are not ready to change right now?
- What is stopping you?
- What will it take to start making that change?
- How will starting it change your life?
- What attributes of this state do you have that you are proud to own?

- How have those attributes helped your life?
- Where do you think you learned them?
- How has *not* having a balanced Nurturing Parent state hurt your life?
- How will balancing your Nurturing Parent state change your life?

Now that you have evaluated your Nurturing Parent, here are a few simple HINTS ON HOW TO BALANCE YOUR NURTURING PARENT.

<u>If your NP is too high</u>:
- Ask yourself, are you mothering or smothering someone?
- Don't offer your assistance; wait until someone asks for help.
- Practice saying no sometimes!
- Try nurturing YOURSELF *before* nurturing others.
- Realize SELF-CARE IS NOT SELFISH.

<u>If your Nurturing Parent is too low</u>:
- Practice giving instead of receiving.
- Practice giving compliments instead of criticism.
- Practice giving up control to others.
- Practice genuine tolerance instead of judgment.
- Practice self-care without judgment.

REBELLIOUS/FREE CHILD

NEGATIVE ATTRIBUTES	POSITIVE ATTRIBUTES
No I Won't!	Rocks Boat For Change
All About Me!	Not Guilt Driven
I Don't Care!	Stands Up For Self
Very Emotional	Has A Voice!
Overly Impulsive	Creative
Few Boundaries	Free Spirited
Too Free Spirited	Light Hearted
Action/No Fear Of	Spontaneous
	Of Consequences

What are three small things you can change to balance your Rebellious/Free Child state?

1.

2.

3.

What are three bigger things you would like to WORK ON CHANGING about your Rebellious/Free Child state?

1.

2.

3.

Journal Questions:
- How will changing these things make you feel about yourself?
- In what way will making these changes have an impact on your life?
- What is some attribute you have that you are not ready to change right now?
- What is stopping you?

91

- What will it take to start making that change?
- How will starting it change your life?
- What attributes of this state do you have that you are proud to own?
- How have those attributes helped your life?
- Where do you think you learned them?
- How has *not* having a balanced Rebellious/Free Child state hurt your life?
- How will balancing your Rebellious/Free Child State change your life?

Now that you have evaluated your Rebellious/Free Child, here are a few simple HINTS ON HOW TO BALANCE YOUR REBELLIOUS/FREE CHILD.

If your R/FC is too high:
- Practice controlling your rebellious behavior; get help if you need it.
- Practice saying YES instead of NO.
- Practice making the world about OTHERS rather than SELF.
- Practice sharing and cooperating with others.
- Look at the possible consequences of your actions BEFORE you take them.

If your R/FC is too low:
- Try asking, "What's in it for ME?"
- Try making your needs as important as the needs of others.
- Try thinking outside the box for answers, behaviors, and new paths.
- Look for and try a new creative outlet.
- Try to find "fun" things to bring your life into balance.

ADAPTIVE CHILD

NEGATIVE ATTRIBUTES	POSITIVE ATTRIBUTES
HELPLESS	ADAPTABLE TO CHANGE
SUBMISSIVE	NOT TOO INVESTED IN RESULT
SEEKS APPROVAL	TRUSTING
GUILT DRIVEN	ADMITS WHEN WRONG
NEVER GETS ANGRY	ABLE TO ASK FOR HELP
TOO VULNERABLE	

What are three small things you can change to balance your Adaptive Child state?

1.

2.

3.

What are three bigger things you would like to WORK ON CHANGING about your Adaptive Child state?

1.

2.

3.

Journal Questions:
- How will changing these things make you feel about yourself?
- In what way will making these changes have an impact on your life?
- What is some attribute you have that you are not ready to change right now?
- What is stopping you?
- What will it take to start making that change?
- How will starting it change your life?
- What attributes of this state do you have that you are proud to own?

- How have those attributes helped your life?
- Where do you think you learned them?
- How has *not* having a balanced Adaptive Child state hurt your life?
- How will balancing your Adaptive Child state change your life?

Now that you have evaluated your Nurturing Parent, here are a few simple HINTS ON HOW TO BALANCE YOUR ADAPTIVE CHILD.

If your AC is too high:
- Try not to look to others for approval.
- Do not use guilt as motivation or as your *modus operandi*.
- Start speaking up about your needs.
- Try making one day about YOU.
- Don't hide your feelings to please others.
- Validate your own needs and desires as WORTHY.
- Try solving your own problems without asking for help.

If your AC is too low:
- Practice saying, "I'm sorry."
- Try listening first to others' needs before your own.
- Practice following instead of leading.
- Let others be the center of attention.

ADULT

NEGATIVE ATTRIBUTES	POSITIVE ATTRIBUTES
I'M THINKING	OBJECTIVE
TOO ANALYTICAL	GOOD ON THE JOB
TOO UNEMOTIONAL	BALANCED DECISION-MAKING
NOT SPONTANEOUS	BALANCED EMOTIONS
DECISIONS BASED ON LOGIC	USES LOGIC TO ADVANTAGE, NOT FEELINGS.

What are three small things you can change to balance your Adult state?

1.

2.

3.

What are three bigger things you would like to WORK ON CHANGING about your Adult state?

1.

2.

3.

Journal Questions:
- How will changing these things make you feel about yourself?
- In what way will making these changes have an impact on your life?
- What is some attribute you have that you are not ready to change right now?
- What is stopping you?
- What will it take to start making that change?
- How will starting it change your life?

- What attributes of this state do you have that you are proud to own?
- How have those attributes helped your life?
- Where do you think you learned them?
- How has *not* having a balanced Adult state hurt your life?
- How will balancing your Adult state change your life?

These journaling questions for all the states can be answered over and over again for the rest of your life!

Now that you have evaluated your Adult, here are a few simple HINTS ON HOW TO BALANCE YOUR ADULT STATE.

If your ADULT state is too high:
- Acknowledge your feelings as much as your thoughts.
- Acknowledge OTHERS' feelings with compassion instead of logic.
- Don't let decisions be solely guided by logic. Let your emotions have some say in the decision process.
- Let go of some rules in favor of FUN.
- Allow spontaneity into your life.

If your Adult state is too small:
- Calm your emotions down with logic and reasoning.
- Allow guidelines and rules to play a larger part in your decision-making.
- Learn to schedule more of your life to balance the spontaneity.

This chapter is truly the beginning of piecing it all together. By now you should have come to the glorious conclusion that your happiness is not as dependent on others as you thought it was. Hopefully, you have realized that YOU have as big a role to play as others do in making or breaking the relationships in your life. You realize that the more you bring your own health into balance, the easier it is to be in a healthy relationship. Hopefully, you have seen what got you here and what you need to change.

The beauty now is that as you become healthier, you attract healthier people into your life! You see the red flags of unhealthy behavior in others and you go the other way. You see your own red flags of old defense mechanisms and imbalances and catch yourself before you get hurt or hurt others. You have been "guy free . . . working on me," but now you can start anew and look for that person who *partners* with you instead of fixing you. Having found your own soul, you are ready to look for your soul mate!

Chapter 14

My Life-Long Journey

THE BEAUTY OF THE human spirit is that we are constantly growing and always changing. The fact that you picked this book up in the first place meant you wanted to be on the road to self-discovery. Hopefully, these chapters have given you insight into yourSELF that will help you along the path of becoming the most genuine you. You *can* break free of your conditioning. You *can* let go of the defenses and communication habits that kept you stuck. You *can* use your new insight to see the red flags in a relationship before it gets out of hand! You *can* watch your old relationship patterns disappear. You *can* change your life, balance your life, and heal your life! Your time is NOW! Time for a new thought process, using new tools, creating a new lifestyle, and living in a new consciousness!

Through these chapters you have been given a map to the deepest and most beautiful parts of your psyche. You have paddled through rivers of your heart and sailed through uncharted places in your soul. You have dug deep and hopefully healed some wounds. The rest of your journey lies ahead. But this time—today, tomorrow, and forever—YOU are at the helm. You have begun "the never-ending fantastical journey of ME."

I wish you smooth sailing and fair winds!
Bon voyage,
Shauna

CPSIA information can be obtained at www.ICGtesting.com
Printed in the USA
LVOW13s2004060913

351185LV00001B/4/P